T4-AKL-065
3 2528 10808 0021

A History of
Foreign Language
Testing
in the United States

from its beginnings to the present

Bilingual Press/Editorial Bilingüe

General Editor
Gary D. Keller

Managing Editor
Karen S. Van Hooft

Associate Editors
Karen M. Akins
Barbara H. Firoozye

Assistant Editor
Linda St. George Thurston

Editorial Consultant
Ingrid Muller

Address:
Bilingual Review/Press
Hispanic Research Center
Arizona State University
P.O. Box 872702
Tempe, Arizona 85287-2702
(602) 965-3867

A History of Foreign Language Testing in the United States

from its beginnings to the present

David Patrick Barnwell

Bilingual Press/Editorial Bilingüe
TEMPE, ARIZONA

© 1996 by Bilingual Press/Editorial Bilingüe

All rights reserved. No part of this publication may be reproduced in any manner without permission in writing, except in the case of brief quotations embodied in critical articles and reviews.

ISBN 0-927534-59-2

Library of Congress Cataloging-in-Publication Data

Barnwell, David Patrick.
    A history of foreign language testing in the United States : from its beginnings to the present / David Patrick Barnwell.
        p.   cm.
    Includes bibliographical references (p.).
    ISBN 0-927534-59-2 (paper : alk. paper)
    1. Language and languages—Ability testing—United States—History. I. Title.
    P53.4.B37   1996
    418'.0076—dc20   96-28087
                                                            CIP

PRINTED IN THE UNITED STATES OF AMERICA

Cover design by John Wincek

Contents

Preface

In 1925 William Barlow, in his annual president's address to the American Association of Teachers of Spanish, warned his audience that the history of modern language teaching in the United States was full of examples of fads. "However, I believe that most of our fads have been important matters imperfectly understood rather than trivial fancies irrationally urged. Many of our fads have been real ideas newborn, but sent forth to revolutionize the field before they had reached maturity and could realize the modest place they were fit to occupy" (1926, 31).

Unlike other fields of human endeavor, foreign language pedagogy preserves but a superficial memory of its own history and benefits little from the patrimony of the great figures of its past. The ideas and labors of those who dominated the profession decades ago go forgotten, and the contributions they made have been erased from memory. When the profession stumbles across questions posed by previous generations, it considers them oblivious to their historical antecedents. The short-term memory views everything as "new" that has not been encountered in the past decade or two. Beyond what they remember from their own experiences, even the foremost current researchers in the field often show little awareness of the issues that were confronted and debated before their time. Few ask whether problems presented in today's foreign language testing might be illuminated by the recognition that they were faced if not solved at an earlier date.

Though foreign language testing has come of age in the past decades and is now recognized as a legitimate focus for specialization and inquiry, few histories of the field exist. The present study attempts to fill this lacuna. It charts the evolution of foreign language testing from its earliest manifestation as a coherent activity in the United States almost a century ago to its most current theory and practice. It situates today's testing in its historical environment, both recent and remote, and seeks to record the work of some of the once landmark figures who have labored in the field. The reader will judge how many of the questions faced in the past are still relevant today, and to what extent ideas now current can trace their genesis to long-forgotten books and articles and their distant authors.

An awareness of the tradition in which they work can only be of benefit to those who seek solutions to the perennial problems faced by educators. Foreign language measurement is no exception to this.

1

The Early Years

In the United States, the beginnings of foreign language testing as an activity somewhat discrete from foreign language teaching can be traced to the closing years of the last century. In 1875 Harvard College began to offer admission examinations in the modern languages. At this time the Harvard handbook defined its elementary requirement in French as "the translation at sight of easy French prose. A knowledge of the language itself, rather than of the grammar, is expected; but proficiency in elementary grammar, a good pronunciation, or facility in speaking the language will be accepted as an offset for some deficiency in translation." The brief examination required in French in 1876 consisted of a sixteen-line passage to be translated into English, a few discrete sentences to be translated from English into French, and finally some grammar questions that focused on verb conjugation (Bagster-Collins 1930, 94). In 1878 the New York Regents examination for high school students was inaugurated. From the outset an examination in French was offered. It consisted of translation of a French passage to English, translation of some isolated English sentences to French, and formal questions that called on candidates to state rules or principles of points of French grammar (Frizzle 1950).

In the later years of the century there was considerable heterogeneity between universities as to what they expected incoming students to be able to do in a modern language. The drive to reach some kind of uniformity led to the creation of such groups as the New England Association of Colleges and Preparatory Schools, organized in Boston in 1885, and similar bodies for the Middle Atlantic and North Central states in 1892 and 1895 respectively. In 1892 the National Education Association appointed a Committee of Ten to review the situation of the modern languages in elementary and high schools. This advisory group recommended that modern language study begin in elementary school or, failing that, in the first year of high school. In 1896 the Modern Language Association created a committee to study existing conditions of modern language teaching and make recommendations for improvements in syllabi and teacher training. The report of this MLA committee has a special place in the history of foreign language teaching and testing, because the Committee of Twelve, as it was known, offered some specimen examinations in French and German for college entrance. These provide an indication of what leading authorities in foreign language education deemed good testing practice at the turn of the century.

The elementary French examination described by the committee consisted of translation to and from French. The former comprised sentences such as:

> Here is the pen. Shall I send it to her?
>
> No, do not send it to her. Give it to me.

The influence of the study of classical languages was patent in the passages to be translated:

> Why do we weep for mortals, whose life and character we scarcely know? We always have them before our eyes. Whatever we may think of them, they are surely worthy of our pity.

A large number of questions on French grammar were based on usages and examples in the texts to be translated.

> Give the conjugation (first person singular of each tense) of *se réjouir* and *savoir*.
>
> Write the inflection of *boire* and *faire* in the present indicative, the future of *pouvoir*, present subjunctive of *prendre*.
>
> In what ways may the use of the passive voice be avoided in French?

Intermediate French included translation to English of a poem by Victor Hugo, as well as expositions of formal grammar such as:

> What are the general principles governing the use of the indicative, conditional, and subjunctive moods?

The advanced French model examination called for a translation from Corneille and Voltaire, as well as the writing of fifteen to twenty lines in French about either figure.

The German model examinations were, if anything, even more oriented toward exhibiting explicit grammatical knowledge. Elementary level German offered such questions as:

> Decline throughout the German phrases meaning *The new house; My dear friend.*

Students were to translate passages such as the following:

> Come now, Hedwig, and eat your breakfast. You are not a bird and cannot fly. And, after all, is it not better to be a pretty girl than a stupid bird?

At the intermediate level students were asked questions that tested the ability to conceptualize and articulate metalinguistic knowledge, such as:

> How do the modal auxiliaries differ from ordinary weak verbs, and how from strong verbs?

These examinations responded to the goals of the time. The primary goals of language learning as laid out at the inaugural meeting of the MLA in 1883 were literary and philological (Lodeman 1887). The stress on overt grammatical knowledge—the ability to verbalize rules and exceptions—and the fondness for the translation of sentences so heavily "seeded" with particular grammar points as to be almost ludicrous in meaning, are common in language examinations from the end of the last century. No opportunity was given to the student to create with the language or even to integrate the disparate grammatical elements mechanically. Students were expected to know about the language rather than know the language. The structure of the exams showed the influence of the teaching of Latin and Greek and made no allowance for the fact that French and German were living languages. All instructions were given in English.

The report of the MLA committee was widely respected and often cited in subsequent years. Its recommendations on testing proved influential in the years after their publication. This was particularly visible in the creation of common examinations for university admission. As a response to the great disparity in standards and requirements for admission among the universities of the Northeast, a group of universities came together to form the College Entrance Examination Board in 1900. Initially the examinations so created catered primarily to students who wished to enter one of the New York institutions, Columbia or Barnard. Examinations were offered in nine areas, two of these being German and French. The foreign language examinations devised by the College Board essentially followed the model laid out in the report of the Committee of Twelve, combining some literary translation with the gauging of metalinguistic knowledge by asking students for an explicit discussion of grammatical rules.

The College Board examinations were first given in 1901. Five hundred forty-four students took the examination in French, while 538 took the German test. These figures compared with the 2,000 or so who took the examinations in Latin. No Spanish examination was set in the first year of the College Boards. In the following year a Spanish examination was administered, but only attracted 9 candidates. The elementary French examination of 1901 called for the translation to English of passages such as the following:

> Il s'agissait de franchir la frontière sans éveiller les soupçons. Il descendit a l'avant-dernière station et chercha quelque paysan qui voulut bien le guider. Un boucheron consentit, pour vingt louis, a lui prêter son office. Mais au lieu de le conduire dans la bonne voie, il l'emmena au milieu d'une forêt et lui declara que si la somme n'était pas à l'instant doublée il allait le dénoncer aux autorités. Paul bondit à la

gorge du traitre, le lia solidement à un tronc d'arbre et se résigna a ne plus compter que sur lui-même. Il parvint, après vingt-quatre heures de vagabondage, à atteindre le territoire de Bohème.

The second section of the elementary French examination asked for explicit grammatical knowledge such as:

Refer to their respective infinitives: *naquis, mus, voulus;*

and:

Give a synopsis (second person singular, simple and compound tenses) of *venir* and *se faire.*

The third part was composed of translations of such sentences as:

I never thought of that. But please do not tell it to them nor to anyone else.

Or:

Patriotism is the affection of the brave for their native land.

(Candidates could not avoid any section; all elements had to be attempted.)

The intermediate French examination offered French passages—one of them a poem—for translation into English. There was also a translation from English into French:

That wealth, that variety, that suppleness of imagination had rendered him fit to feel marvelously the works of nature. Bernardin de Saint-Pierre used to say to Madame de Beaumont, half modesty, half archness: "I have only a little brush, M. de Chateaubriand has a big brush." Since we are people who make metaphors, let us allow ourselves to say that Bernardin de Saint-Pierre has a little flute and that Chateaubriand has a whole orchestra, or rather let us say simply that with Lucretius and La Fontaine, Chateaubriand is the greatest painter and the most eloquent interpreter of nature that we know, and that again he is a Lucretius without system, and, as he has travelled, a richer La Fontaine.

This kind of format was not universally admired by language teachers, however, and was to be the source of considerable discontent to them as the years wore on. For one thing, as opposed to other subjects, the College Board set three separate examinations in modern language, Elementary, Intermediate, and Advanced. This gave rise to the festering problem of how to equate performance across the examinations. A student who received a barely passing grade (generally 60 percent) on the advanced paper received three credits, while even the most outstanding performance on the intermediate paper could yield but two. The former could take literature classes at college, whereas the latter could not. Further, teachers who wished to follow one or another of the innovative methodologies of the time, such as the Phonetic Method or the Natural Method, were constrained from doing so by the knowledge that their students would have to pass an examination that was based on a purely formalistic and literary view of language. The universities, where approaches to language teaching were always more conservative than in the high schools, continued to wield their influence to prevent the examinations from keeping up with new developments in the field.

Heuser (1921), in describing examinations in German given during the prewar years, expressed a commonly held attitude: "No amount of declining is worth anything, unless the respective cases can be used in sentences" (190). Though from 1912 onward some instructions on the examination were given in German, the metalinguistic emphasis persisted. One such formalistic question written in German asked students to list six prepositions that govern the accusative. Heuser astutely pointed out that "formal grammar asked in German marks no real progress" (188). For a short time the German examination also included a dictation, read by the teacher, but this practice was dropped shortly after its introduction. Heuser regretted this change and in addition proposed that another auditory test be added that involved the retelling in English of an "anecdote" read by the teacher in German. This suggestion was not adopted. There were some innovations from time to time, such as in 1912, when students were for the first time asked to create with the language by using certain words in original sentences. In 1914 a written composition was introduced. The instructions to students for this were quite vague and left them with a very ill defined task. Candidates were asked to write, in forty to fifty words, "eine kleine Anekdote."

Grammatical formalism and philological emphasis were at their strongest in the teaching and testing of German. The position of French was a little different, with a modicum of effort to integrate the vocabulary and grammar of the language. In 1917 Méras published an analysis of 178 French examinations set by American universities. Ninety-eight percent called for translation from the French; a slightly smaller number required translation in the other direction. A variety of other testing techniques was employed, though each to a much lesser extent than translation. These formats included dictation, questions on readings, and free composition. As in the case of German, a considerable number of discrete grammatical points were dealt with: about 70 percent of the papers asked for explicit conjugation of verb tense paradigms, while time and again such things as noun-adjective concordance, possessive adjectives, and pronouns were tested.

Students were presented with such tasks as:

> Discuss fully the formation of the feminine of adjectives, giving exceptional forms.

Or:

> Give rules for the agreement of past participles.

Or:

> Make a diagram showing the relative position of all personal pronoun objects when standing before the verb.

Or:

How do you choose between *à* and *en* to translate *in* before geographical names?

Méras declared himself opposed to this type of test, especially because of its stress on information about the language rather than on the use of the language itself. He argued that "the candidate should be tested in ability to apply French grammar in the construction of real French sentences, and not in ability to organize grammatical facts in valueless lists and synopses, or in meaningless rules and diagrams." He offered alternative formats for testing the same grammatical points as covered in the examinations. For example, to test past participle agreement, Méras put forward the following:

Copiez le paragraphe suivant et mettez tous les verbes au passé indéfini:

Ce jour-là elle alla aux affaires. Elle rentra tard et se coucha tout de suite. Elle ne dormit que deux heures. Elle se leva pour lire une histoire qu'elle ne comprit pas bien.

To test adjective gender and number:

Mettez au féminin les cinq phrases suivantes et puis mettez les dix phrases au pluriel:

a) L'oncle a acheté un chien pour son petit neveu.

b) Ce beau garçon est plus actif que son frère.

c) Mon vieux grand-père est plus silencieux que le vôtre.

d) Cet homme n'est jamais chez lui.

e) Celui qui est doux n'est pas toujours franc.

Méras's approach to testing depended to a large extent on the technique of having students rewrite sentences or passages or fill in blanks in sentences. In this regard his testing formats remained popular in the United States for many subsequent decades, and indeed are still in quite widespread use.

The writings of critics such as Méras and Burchinall (1916) not only articulate contemporary disquiet with the design of important foreign language examinations, but in them one also witnesses the beginning of a concept of language testing as a discrete activity, one with its own internal set of desiderata, logic, and values. The nascent interest in foreign language testing was in keeping with a general explosion of interest in testing of all kinds. The early years of the century saw the beginnings of the great movement directed toward the measurement of human differences. In 1904 E. L. Thorndike published the monumental *Introduction to the Theory of Mental and Social Measurements*, perhaps the first book solely devoted to the topic of educational or psychological measurement. Binet's pioneer work with intelligence testing in Europe became known in the United States in 1910, when Goddard published an adaptation of the Binet test to American conditions. The more famous Stanford revision of the Binet Scale came some years later (Terman 1916). The first report of an attempt to draw up a standardized test of a particular school subject comes in 1908 with Stone's arithmetic test. This was followed by an increasing stream of tests and scales for the measurement of such diverse things as handwriting, drawing ability, and spelling.

Though the First World War in some ways slowed the acceleration in educational research, in another way it gave impetus to the great movement in testing. The U.S. Army, faced with the need to classify its hundreds of thousands of recruits and place them in services where their talents might be used to best advantage, sought tests that could be administered to groups rather than individuals. The military turned to the work of psychological testers such as Otis (1918) and Yerkes (1921), and the result was the creation of the army Alpha and Beta tests. Indispensable in these tests was the work of Frederick Kelly, the inventor of the multiple-choice test. Kelly's Silent Reading Test (1915) represented the first published multiple-choice test in any subject. It offered questions such as:

Below are given the names of four animals. Draw a line around the name of each animal that is useful on the farm:

cow   tiger   rat   wolf

Kelly's format permitted testing to be carried out on a vast scale; tests could be quickly and easily scored by low-level clerical workers whose only technology was the superimposed stencil. It came to define an entire educational system and set the United States apart from Europe.

In addition, the army fostered what were termed "man-to-man" rating scales, in which officers were asked to make judgments to differentiate between enlisted men's particular strengths and weaknesses. Tests, not just of intelligence but of a wide range of vocational abilities, were administered in all to perhaps two million men in the U.S. military.

Once peace was declared, the energy of educators and psychologists became truly liberated. The years around the close of the First World War and after witnessed an unprecedented expansion in the quantity of educational inquiry. Journals such as *Hispania* (1917) and *The Journal of Educational Research* (1920) were founded. For the first time teacher education courses began to include lectures on statistics, with H. O. Rugg's *Statistical Methods Applied to Education* (1917) becoming widely studied. The number of doctoral degrees granted in education rose from 53 in 1918 to 94 in 1923 to 189 in 1927. The quantity of other research reports published on education rose correspondingly, from 165 in 1918 to 333 in 1927 (Monroe 1928, 46). Research institutions began to spring up on all sides. The Iowa Child Welfare Research Station, set up in 1917 at the University of Iowa, the Bureau of Educational Research at the University of Illinois, established in 1918, Teachers College Institute of Educational Research, founded in New York in 1922, all were to play a major role in the burgeoning research movement. More public bodies concerned with research were also created. The American Council on Education was founded in 1918; the Research Department of the National Education Association was instituted four years later. Supportive financing was made available through bodies such as the Carnegie Foundation and the Russell Sage Foundation. Funding was available for research in education, because it was "relatively easy to secure financial assistance for a clearly defined project" (Monroe 1928, 51).

The war had effected a fundamental change in the pattern of foreign language study in the United States. The anti-German attitudes that sprang up as a result of political and military enmity could not fail to permeate the educational system. German, for so long the most commonly taught language, in the public systems at any rate, fell into a chasm from which it was never fully to escape. Before the war about 25 percent of all public school pupils had been taking German. In 1921-22 the figure was less than 1 percent. Where French had always been strong, as in the Northeast and South, and especially in the private schools, it picked up much of the slack. Elsewhere, particularly in the West, and throughout the public schools, Spanish enjoyed dramatically increased enrollments. All of this happened against a background of rapidly growing high school attendance generally. In 1898 there were about six hundred thousand pupils enrolled in U.S. high schools, with around ninety thousand in universities and colleges. By 1918 this had risen to more than two and a half million in the high schools and almost three hundred thousand in colleges or universities (Henmon 1925, 7). The exponential increase persisted until well into the 1920s, especially at the high school level (F. Phillips 1928). The hitherto semiexclusive doors of the high schools had been democratically thrown open to all. Millions of pupils were now coming into the expanded high school system. Schools were swamped by large increases in student numbers, and the student body was becoming much more heterogeneous than before. The educational system was thus faced with teaching large numbers of children who were dissimilar in background to those the schools had been used to. High schools were no longer seen as mere feeder institutions for elitist universities. Rather, they were viewed as offering an education that was intrinsically worthwhile, especially in view of the vastly increased numbers and variety of backgrounds of those in attendance.

In 1925 there were approximately twenty thousand public schools in the United States. About half of these—generally the larger and more urban schools—offered one or more modern languages. About one in six taught no language, either foreign or classical, at all. The remainder taught Latin, or much more rarely, Greek. While many schools offered Latin but no modern language, it was very rare to find a school that offered a modern language but no Latin. Latin was thus well ahead of all other languages, being almost as strong in terms of enrollment as all modern languages combined, especially in rural and smaller schools. There were about three quarters of a million enrollments in modern languages, in a total secondary enrollment of almost three million. The actual number of students studying foreign languages must have been less, because there were some duplicate enrollments. Although the exact number is not available, it is clear that only a minority of high school students—probably fewer than 20 percent—was enrolled in modern language classes. In terms of percentages, languages had thus lost some ground; put another way, they were underrepresented among the new wave of high school students. One of the elements that had brought this about was that in the Midwest, the traditional center of German study, no language had supplanted German after its postwar decline.

A survey taken in 1925 found that about 83 percent of students of foreign languages in the high schools (public and private) went no further than completing two years of study. Fifty-seven percent went no further than finishing their first year. Third-year registration in modern languages was about 16 percent of that of the first-year enrollment, and fourth-year registration was a mere 2 percent of that of the first year (Wheeler 1928). As Coleman put it (1929, 27),

> In fact there appears to prevail in public school circles the judgment, implied if nowhere definitely formulated, that the normal course in a foreign language, ancient or modern, should last only two years if the student's general secondary education is to be provided for properly. This probably . . . results from more recent tendencies in curriculum revision in

behalf of the large groups of young people who formerly did
not enter the secondary school.

Another important factor was that of late starters. About
one-fifth of beginners in language courses was already in the
eleventh grade and had therefore at most two years in which,
in Coleman's words, "to develop the language power and to
cultivate the attitudes by which the contribution of the subject
to their education will be chiefly determined." Short exposure
to foreign languages was institutionalized by the fact that there
were a large number of schools that offered only two years of
French or Spanish, and quite a few that offered only one year.
Throughout the system, attrition rates, or "discontinuance" as
it was called at the time, for modern languages were twice that
for the schools as a whole. In fact, though the numbers of junior high schools and the student population were growing
rapidly, teaching modern languages at junior high schools
appeared to be a complete waste of time due to the problem of
discontinuance.

This had a "knock-on effect" at the college level, where
there was much "lost motion," to use another then-current
term, in the transfer from high school. Here the strengths and
weaknesses of high school enrollment patterns were to some
extent reversed. At the college level Latin had lost its pre-emi-
nent place by the 1920s. Proportionately more college students took foreign languages than did those in high school.
Beginning German was especially popular, because anti-
German sentiment had caused it to be dropped from most
high schools since the war.

Against this background there emerged a clear and pressing
need for educational research. This inevitably heightened the
interest in measurement, because a fundamental requirement
for research was the ability to quantify its outcomes. Monroe
(1928) calculated that some thirteen hundred different educational and psychological tests and scales were produced between 1918 and 1927. At the time of his writing, in 1927-28,
he estimated that no fewer than 30 million copies of standard-

ized or semistandardized tests were being used in the United States each year. It was not uncommon for sales of tests in the more popular areas such as mathematics or reading to approach a million copies per year. There were published tests and scales for rating everything, from the quality of maintenance of school buildings to the performance of clergymen or the "school habits" of children. The famous psychologist Thurstone himself developed a "rhythm test" to predict the speed of future telegraphers (Wainer 1990, 6). The Scholastic Aptitude Tests made their first appearance in 1926; significantly, the College Entrance Examination Board had decided to employ a multiple-choice format. The Iowa High School Testing Program began in 1929—the first statewide testing system. The army itself contributed to the testing boom by dumping its vast supplies of psychological tests on the postwar civilian market.

Inevitably, foreign language testing participated in the great testing wave and shared its preferred formats. As early as 1916, a series of language tests was published by Charles Starch as part of his book *Educational Measurements*. These tests were of a type hitherto not seen and were quite dissimilar to those put out by the College Board. The examination consisted of two parts, a vocabulary test and a translation test. Starch based his vocabulary test on a list of one hundred words taken at random from a foreign language dictionary. In the case of German these were the first words of every twenty-third page, with twenty-three being merely the frequency of selection needed in order to yield one hundred words. Students were provided with two lists of one hundred words, one in English and the other in the target language. They had to match each foreign word with its English "equivalent."

Starch defended his method by pointing out that it provided a comprehensive random sample of vocabulary. He maintained that a score on his test would indicate the percentage of words in the entire foreign language vocabulary that a person knew. "If a pupil knows 25 words of each list it means that he knows 25 percent of the entire vocabulary."

However, the very randomness of the word selection method confounded common sense; it meant that the entire dictionary range of target language frequency and register was encountered, with no attempt to graduate for frequency of use in the spoken or even written language. Thus, in the French test, words such as *condylien, cophrophage, regreffer, chrysocal,* and *emmitoufler* were given, along with such everyday words as *avoir, jeter, bas,* and *scientifique.* As one contemporary critic put it, "It tested a promiscuous vocabulary, which we do not seek to teach" (Handschin 1920, 220).

Starch's translation test consisted of thirty target language sentences, ranged in what he presumed to be an increasing order of difficulty. He demonstrated no awareness of the grading problems that need to be addressed before translation can be reliably evaluated. The translation was either entirely right or entirely wrong. Further, Starch's tests did not differentiate between modern and ancient languages; the examination format for French and German followed the one he offered for Latin. For reasons such as these, Starch's work had little influence, and foreign language testing had to wait some time before taking its great leaps forward.

The first standardized modern language test was Charles Handschin's *Silent Reading Test in French and Spanish* (1919). Handschin, who was on the faculty of Ohio's Miami University, may deserve the title of America's first foreign language tester, for he was the first person to think in terms of general principles of testing, as well as look to experimental results. In describing his test (1920), he set out eight principles for the construction of a foreign language test, the most comprehensive such list drawn up to that date. These were:

1. The test must be objective. "Half a dozen or any number of teachers administering the test separately will each get the same reaction and the same score."

2. "It must test in a manner analogous to the one usually employed by teachers, and not in a way in which classes have never reacted before."

3. It must be valuable to teacher and student from the start, i.e., even before it is standardized.

4. It must be comprehensive enough to include all from the poorest to the best students.

5. The units of the scale must not be too large or too small.

6. It must be tested out in several thousand cases, at least.

7. It must be simple, so that teacher and student will not waste time attempting to learn what is wanted.

8. The method of administering and of scoring must be simple and require very little time.

Handschin's French test included a paragraph of 192 words with ten questions, to be answered in either English or French, as well as a comprehension and grammar test based on completions and inflections. This test was followed by Vivion Henmon's *French Test of Vocabulary and Sentence Translation* in 1921. Henmon had earlier published a test for Latin, and his French test followed the same format. It consisted of 60 French words and twelve sentences given in supposed order of difficulty. Students had to translate contextless French words and phrases into English. The entire test, though not explicitly speeded, was expected to take about twenty minutes. An attempt was made to control the level of difficulty of the vocabulary, with all words used being taken from first-year texts. The problem of rater reliability, however, was not addressed; no pointers as to scoring were given, except to score "right" or "wrong" without giving partial credit. Scoring could be carried out by a simple count or by using weighted scores on the basis of supposed levels of difficulty.

Though he knew French, Henmon was not a language teacher; he was a testing specialist, and his tests often showed a lack of appreciation for what is important in a foreign language. The parallel between Henmon's Latin test and his French test is significant, because it shows that no specific methodology for testing the vernacular aspects of modern languages had yet been devised. Even though his testing was innovative and represented the most modern approach at that time, Henmon did not attempt to assess the spoken language, nor did he devise any structure for modern language testing that would differentiate it from the testing of the ancient languages.

In 1915 the State University of New York (SUNY) instituted "examinations for oral credit" to be given to prospective foreign language teachers. These examinations provide details about foreign language testing practices at more advanced levels of ability. In the French examination of October 1916, candidates were provided with a long passage in French by George Sand and were asked to engage in a series of text-based exegetic exercises. This format was quite typical of the time, when it was common to base the drill and grammar activities of a whole class on a limited written text. In the SUNY examination, a comprehensive set of exercises was given, all based on the text provided. First, students were to give a written description of the pronunciation of twenty specified words from the text, preferably using phonetic notation. This, too, was common in the language classroom of the time, in accordance with Henry Sweet's *The Practical Study of Language* (1899), in which he called for the teaching of phonetic notation as a prerequisite to language instruction. Second, candidates were to explain thirty specified words, either by French synonyms/antonyms or by definitions in French. Third, they were given twenty words from the text to be used in original sentences, to show that they understood the meaning of these words. Finally, they wrote a composition on a subject suggested by the text. As was then typical, no specific title was provided for this composition—candidates could deal with "any subject." If the use of open-ended essay topics created difficulties in reliably evaluating what candidates wrote, there was no suggestion of this at the time (Decker 1917).

The sentences posed for translation bore little relation to normal discourse. They were heavily seeded with grammar, with little concern for meaning or context.

> I want some tea, do you want any? No, I have some yet.

And:

> Children are happy everywhere. Even without money and without friends they are happy.

The success rate in the examination was quite high—in 1916 about 75 percent of candidates passed. Though this was purely a written test, the oral component was not overlooked in the certification of teachers in New York. Those who passed the written exam were still subject to classroom observation, and permanent approval was denied those teachers "whose work in the classroom showed their inability to use the language orally" (Decker 1917, 126). No details were given as to what kind of a classroom test would be used to yield this information.

Few tests in use at that time sought to assess the spoken language, even though elements within the profession had been aware of this deficiency for a long time. In the first decade of the twentieth century the New England Modern Language Association, a body closely linked to the College Board, on several occasions addressed the question of how oral work was to be evaluated and rewarded. In 1915 a committee of the Modern Language Association recommended that those aspiring to college admission be required to pass a test in auditory comprehension. The recommended format for this examination was to be a dictation followed by written answers to questions spoken by the examiner in the foreign language. A third element called for a kind of translation, in which a student had to reproduce in English a passage he had heard in the foreign language. Some Ivy League institutions, such as Columbia (Hayden 1920), Cornell, and Princeton (Decker 1925), adopted this test for use at the entrance level. Later, the University of Utah followed a similar format (Lundeberg 1929).

Fleagle (1923) described auditory tests used in North Carolina. These included some conversational-type questions, with students writing their answers in the foreign language. However, they did not form any coherent train of discourse; in the Spanish test, after a series of questions on the candidate's family, the last question given in the list was

¿Dónde hay más ingleses, en Italia o en Inglaterra?

In reading the literature of the time, it is worth treating the term "oral" with caution, because for a long time the term was sloppily used. Most contemporary writers used the term "oral tests" to refer to what today would be called "auditory" or "listening" tests. The only aspect of true oral expression to receive any attention in the early 1920s was pronunciation. Invariably it was French pronunciation that was tested; German and Spanish pronunciation were ignored. Arthur Bovée (1925) describes a pronunciation test used at the University of Chicago. The students were required to read a paragraph aloud three times, being scored each time. Bovée believed (erroneously) that all the important sounds of French were contained in the sentence. The test was economical, requiring about two minutes per student. The sentence reported by Bovée was

Tout le monde sait une chose—c'est que quand on est doux on ne meurt pas de faim, car l'on donne à l'autre de quoi se tirer d'affaire.

As can be seen, the effort to cover the widest possible range of the sounds of French gave rise to the creation of a nonsensical sentence. Hayden (1920) articulated an objection to oral testing that has often been reheard in subsequent decades. Hayden could not see how "a general conversation test" could be administered rapidly to large numbers. In any case, he maintained that such a test would not yield any information that had not already been produced by other tests. Robert (1926, 20) wrote that oral work "for the mere sake of being able to converse in French is a Berlitz ideal beyond which we should go."

Despite such attitudes to oral testing, it would be fallacious to conclude that the profession, or at least its most self-conscious and innovative wings, was at this time unconcerned about oral goals. Indeed, Hayden himself described an oral examination, basically an interpretation test, in which the candidate interpreted from one of two examiners to the other. This type of test had already been used for some years in civil service examinations (Lundeberg 1929, 196). Though the earliest decades of this century were marked by skepticism about the feasibility of oral testing, many writers saw the value of oral ability, but only as one of several objectives of foreign language study.

There is no need to offer an extended critique of the testing instruments in use in the early 1920s and before. Efforts such as those sketched here represent the beginnings of the language testing tradition in the United States and should be evaluated as such, rather than being subjected to criteria that might be used in assessing tests that purport to be useful for today. In the early 1920s those involved in teaching for the first time were consciously reflecting on the question of how to assess achievement and in doing so, were actually creating the very idea of foreign language testing as an academic activity. From this time onward the notion that the creation and evaluation of language tests is a business intrinsically worthy of debate and study has been accepted within foreign language pedagogy in the United States. This part of the American tradition contrasts with that of Europe, where on the whole interest in foreign language testing is much more recent.

The deficiencies of the early tests described here were as apparent to many of their contemporaries as they are today. In the mid-1920s major advances were made in the effort to put testing on a rational, even scientific basis. Commentators had for years pointed out the inconsistencies in grading the "old-type" examinations, whether caused by subjectivity of standards or mere carelessness. Ill-defined and capricious weighting systems as to relative difficulty levels or importance of particular topics caused standards to change from examination to examination. Critics argued that the small number of questions on the old-type tests made a misunderstanding of the question or ignorance of one topic all the more disastrous. It was charged that the essay-type question wasted time for both examinee and examiner, because only a proportion of the essay would be truly "relevant" to the establishment of the candidate's level.

Since their inception in 1900 the College Boards had always had a significant unreliability problem. An examination of passing rates on the nine College Boards subject examinations between 1910 and 1919 shows that French was in second place, with a rate of 62 percent. German was second to last, with a passing rate of 50 percent. Those who took the French examination were either better prepared, or, as was believed at the time, grading norms were more lax in their case. Standards oscillated from year to year; in 1916, 73 percent passed intermediate French, in 1917 only 42 percent. In 1926, 53 percent passed the French examination, while the percentage rose to 82 percent the following year. In 1931, 58 percent passed, increasing to 82 percent the following year (Kandel 1936, 52).

It is hard to account for these disparities on the basis of differences in student abilities from year to year. Rather, it can be supposed that the oscillations were due to differences in the difficulty level of the examination or severity of grading. Great importance could accrue to the examiners' choice of translation topics and vocabulary. If the theme of the passage for translation was one with which students were familiar, achievement improved dramatically. Good performance on the translation was in itself almost sufficient to ensure a pass on the examination as a whole. The text for translation was set at a formal or uncolloquial register. For instance the French to English passage never used the "passé composé," opting instead for the "passé défini." In addition, the composition test was short, requiring only 125 to 150 words. A wide choice of titles was given. In the 1927 French examination the subject of the composition was:

> Une journée d'une des personnes suivantes, racontée à la première personne: un médecin, un employé de banque, un voyageur de commerce, un fermier, un épicier, une mère de famille, une vendeuse de grand magasin, une actrice.

In some cases the examination scores of the College Boards were challenged by the universities, and the Boards were consequently sensitive to questions of unreliability of scoring. The eighteenth annual report of the College Board contained a detailed description of how grading was carried out and what steps were taken to foster uniformity of marking standards. During the grading period the "readers"—many of them visitors to New York—were encouraged to live and eat together. The undertaking had the character of an "educational congress," in which the readers "live in close proximity, many of them in the same building, and they usually take their meals together." Here began the tradition of hermetic, even hothouse grading sessions that survives today in the practice of Advanced Placement grading sessions.

The report contained a long description of the grading procedures used in French:

> With copies of the examination before us, the chief reader asks all of us to suggest ratings for the several questions as a whole. These suggestions are tabulated, and after a free discussion we come to a conclusion. Then each separate sentence of both translations is given its rating, and a value is placed on every minute point of the grammar question.

Once a common standard was hammered out, the grading began. Four or five readers would read the same answer book, and in the case of any wide discrepancy of marking "there is more careful consultation and discussion, with the chief reader acting as moderator." Readers who were native speakers of French were paired off with native speakers of English, as was the case with new and experienced readers. Papers at the high and low ends of the spectrum were given special attention; if necessary, the group as a whole took the time to review a problematic case. The entire process, though laborious, was apparently quite efficient, because two examiners could get through as many as ninety papers in their six-hour day. The report saw no logic in the practice of some universities of having their own faculty regrade the examinations later in the summer. With some reason it pointed out that if the regrading examiners followed the same standards as initially set there was no justification for the rereading. If the new examiners had different standards, they should have been present at the original examiners' meeting to argue for these standards.

2

The Testing Wave

Examinations such as those of the College Board represented what was known as the "old type" of format. In the 1920s the supremacy of such designs was challenged by the "new-type" examination. This essentially represented the application to the classroom of the kinds of instruments that had already been created for standardized tests such as those for intelligence. In E. L. Thorndike's words (1928),

> Very important work has shown that the selection of the best response from a number of responses presented to the person tested often does nearly or quite as well as the creation of a response by him. This seems to be the case, for example, in tests of comprehension of paragraphs and of the completion of sentences, if sufficient genius and labor is expended in finding or devising the alternatives for selection.

Initially, the true/false scoring method was most popular, but as the 1920s wore on, multiple-choice, matching, completion, correct-the-error, rearrangement, and other formats were added to the tester's repertoire. The required response was in all cases brief: a check mark, a number, a word, or at most a few words. Translation and, to some extent, composition were eschewed in favor of discrete chunks of language—individual words or short sentences. Sampling was wide, since many topics could be introduced. The examination could be comprehensive in scope and in level of complexity, as perhaps fifty or more questions were asked where previously merely a handful had been posed. The element of chance was thus diminished, offering the promise of higher reliability levels.

The ease and economy of grading for the new-type tests were of course offset by the much greater complexity involved in the preparation of such tests; in this respect they were the opposite of the old-type examinations. Rather than, for instance, asking students to write an essay on any topic they wished, questions for the new-type tests required careful and time-consuming elaboration. However, at a time of rapid increase in numbers of students and, consequently, of papers to be marked, the consideration of ease of scoring was predominant. On a broader level, the new tendency in testing reflected evolving structures in society at large. The new types of students flocking through the high schools required a new kind of test.

Wood's New York Experiment

In the general enthusiasm for testing in all subjects it was not uncommon for enormous numbers of students to be tested on the same day. One vast project in modern languages was undertaken in New York City (Wood 1927). Availing themselves of funds from the Carnegie Foundation, the board of education of the city and the regents of the State University of New York administered experimental new-type tests to the city's high school students. These tests were based to a significant extent on pilot work that had been carried on in placement testing at Columbia College in New York. Ben Wood, associate professor at Columbia College, was the principal designer of the tests. Wood had studied at Columbia under Thorndike and had served as an army psychologist during the war. As early as 1923 he had been instrumental in the setting up of a Bureau of Educational Research at Columbia, to improve measurement and guidance. The creation of this kind of body in a liberal arts institution such as Columbia shows the importance attached to testing and placement questions during the 1920s. Through the bureau Wood attempted to bring new testing formats even to such venerable courses of study at Columbia as law and medicine.

Wood undertook to test all the modern language pupils in the junior high schools of New York city for two successive years, 1925 and 1926, and in the high schools to test all those who took the 1925 Regents examination. An experimental form of the Regents examination given at the senior level was taken by over thirty-one thousand foreign language students in 1925. The other test, that for junior high school students, was administered in both 1925 and 1926. Some nineteen thousand students of French took this test during each of the two years; about six thousand five hundred took the Spanish test in 1925 and about four thousand in 1926. The format of the new-type tests made it possible for the first time to compare achievements between schools and between classes in the same school.

Contrary to traditional practice, the tests were not fine-tuned in respect to the year of study. The junior test was given to junior high school students, regardless of whether they were in their first or second year. The senior examination was given to students at any point in the senior cycle. Each test took ninety minutes.

The junior tests, given in French and Spanish, followed almost identical formats in the two languages. They were composed of three parts. Part 1 consisted of one hundred target language words, each followed by five English words. The words were selected, as so often at the time, from the most common words in contemporary word lists. The student chose the "equivalent" English word for the foreign term.

> *chien*
> 1. chin   2. Chinese   3. dog   4. shine   5. cat
>
> *zapato*
> 1. leather   2. spade   3. shoe   4. club   5. strike

Part 2 was a reading comprehension test. Sixty incomplete statements were given in the target language, with five alternative endings. The students' task was to pick the ending that was "coherent or true."

On se sert d'encre pour

1. manger   2. boire   3. courir   4. nager   5. écrire

El perro normal tiene

1. una cabeza   2. cinco pies   3. un reloj   4. tres orejas
5. cincuenta años

Grammar was the focus for part 3, which was composed of sixty English sentences, each followed by an incomplete target language translation. The student was required to complete the translation.

Her dress is white.

Sa robe ___.

I am 12 years old.

___ doce años.

Wood believed that these tests represented a fundamental improvement over old-style translation or composition tests. They were the products of sustained work in pretesting and norming over a long period and thus shared none of the "casualness" he associated with earlier approaches. The vocabulary of the new-style tests, based as it was on word counts for elementary French and Spanish, was, he felt, more rationally chosen than heretofore and constituted a broad sample of the most common words in each language. The multiple-choice format was economical, in Wood's view, for it meant that particular problem areas could be addressed, with little time lost in "irrelevant activities, such as writing out translations of whole sentences or paragraphs." The new exams were comprehensive and proficiency based rather than rooted in particular courses of instruction. They sought to measure outcomes, that is, how much the student had learned, "regardless of whether he learned it from the teacher of that course, or in spite of the teacher." And they took no account of "time-serving," the great bête noire of foreign language teachers even at this time, that is, the practice of rewarding students for the amount of time spent in class or the number of courses taken, rather than giving credit for attained ability irrespective of the time spent in attaining it.

One of the striking elements of the early literature on foreign language testing is the degree to which discussions overlooked the centrality of grading and scoring decisions to the reliability and validity of tests. Ben Wood was unusual for the attention he devoted to problems of scoring. In parts 1 and 2 of the junior high school tests, scoring was quite objective, there being only one acceptable answer. Part 3 was less so, but here directions to scorers were quite stringent: "Absolute correctness must be rigorously enforced; no answer is to receive any credit if it is in any respect—spelling, punctuation, capitalization, etc.—deficient or incomplete." Reliability figures for the junior high school test were high: the reliability coefficient (split half) for the French test as a whole was .97, with similar figures for each constituent part.

Like subsequent foreign language testers, Wood faced the lack of universally accepted external validating criteria for his tests. He believed that it was unnecessary to even argue for the validity of parts 1 and 3 of the tests, since "vocabulary and grammar tests of this sort have been so thoroughly tried out and proved that no scientist or teacher who has kept pace with recent developments can doubt their quality." (The empirical basis for the new tests was of course much more tenuous than might be assumed from such statements.) As scores on the more innovative part 2 correlated well with scores on parts 1 and 3—generally at a coefficient of around .80—Wood argued that this validated part 2. In discussing intercorrelations within a battery and using high values for these as an argument for test validity, Wood showed a tendency to have it both ways, to read into the figures what he wanted them to show. His was the first airing of a topic that even today has not been fully exhausted by foreign language testers, namely, the credence to be placed on correlations between tests. Wood's attitude toward statistics reappears again and again in the history of foreign language testing. The correlations, he wrote, were "high enough to vindicate Part II for general measurement purposes, and low enough to show that it is not a mere duplication of Parts I and III." For Wood, and for many of his successors, separate components of a language test or battery should intercorrelate well but not too well, lest they seem to be redundant. In this Wood was a little oblivious of the limitations of correlation. As subsequent critics of standardized testing have pointed out, the notion that correlation implies a true relationship can be quite fallacious. Stephen Gould (1981) observed that the correlation between his age and rising gas prices would be nearly 1.0. Did this mean that rising gas prices caused him to grow old, or that his growing old caused gas prices to rise?

For the Regents examination Wood showed external validity in the form of fairly high correlations between scores on the test and teachers' grades or scores on the old-type form. He did not address the logical inconsistency involved in validating a new and supposedly superior test against other, often unreliable, measurements that it sets out to supplant. However, Wood did put forward further evidence for the validity of the tests he employed. He showed that the great majority of questions discriminated well, i.e., they were more likely to be answered correctly by good students than bad. Wood's statistical treatment was the first published use of detailed item analysis in evaluating a foreign language test.

Regents Alpha

In the new Regents examination, section 2 was composed of seventy-five true/false statements in the target language "of an obvious truth or obvious fallacy . . . easily within the knowledge of any high school student intelligent enough to study a foreign language." Most of these look unexceptional now, with items that appear to have met this criterion, though a few may have had a rather significant nonlinguistic component:

> El gobernador de un estado es siempre la persona más inteligente del estado.

La Alhambra es un célebre palacio en Granada.

Para leer bien hay que aprender de memoria algunas poesías.

Tous ceux qui habitent la campagne sont des paysans.

On ne voit pas les étoiles quand il y a pleine lune.

Les monuments ne servent à rien.

The practice of intercorrelating scores on the new-type tests with those on the old Regents format was tenable only if reliability figures on both were high. Yet no proper statistical treatments of scores on the old-type examinations existed. Wood therefore analyzed the scorer reliability of a number of old-style Regents examinations from previous years. Of about a thousand scripts each in French and Spanish, he calculated reliabilities between .5 and .78. This compared with reliabilities for the new-type examinations ranging between .8 and .9. The ratings for the old-type Regents examinations varied tremendously from school to school. Wood realized that reliabilities for the old-type examinations were unacceptable, and that they made any correlation between them and the new-type examinations almost meaningless. However, this did not stop him from citing these very correlations as evidence for the validity of his new-type tests. Wood did carry out intercorrelation calculations and found that the new-type correlated with the old-type at values around .6. He considered this figure "satisfactory" and offered it as evidence for the validity of the new-type tests. This figure concealed some wide differences in patterns on the two types of Regents examinations. Students who did well on the new-type failed the old-type examination, and vice versa.

What information did such a vast study as that undertaken in New York yield? The fundamental finding was that efforts at testing and assessment, inasmuch as they existed, were not doing what needed to be done. The standardization that the Regents examination was supposed to impose on the New York school system was totally absent. Wood showed that a vast amount of "overlapping" or misplacement was taking

place. Thousands of students were misplaced by at least a semester, that is, they were nearer in achievement to the average
of the class above or below them than of the class they were
presently taking. Wood called this "the sacrificing of bright
students on the altar of mediocrity" and bemoaned its con-
comitant "wasted energies and frayed nerves." Wide disparities were visible in the achievement of the forty-four individual
schools that took part in the junior high school study, and
even within particular schools. There were violent fluc-
tuations. A fourth-semester class in one school showed average achievement that was little better than that of a third-
semester class in another school. A so-called third-semester
class in one school might have been better termed fourth-
semester, because the average of its scores met or exceeded the
citywide fourth-semester average. The reverse was equally
likely—a so-called third-semester class being actually a misnomer for a true second-semester class, based on citywide aver-
ages. Such disparities could also exist within the same school.
Only about 40 percent of second-semester students of French
were closer to the average of their own class than to some
other class average. The position was even worse for Spanish.
Because of haphazard placement, Wood observed, teachers
did not "have classes to teach but heterogeneous aggregations
of unhappy students."

No improvement as to homogeneity of levels of language
instruction was noticeable between 1925 and 1926. If anything, there was deterioration all around; misplacement had
become even more rife, particularly in Spanish, and many of
the schools or classes scoring well in 1925 had slipped back.
The relation between first- and second-year outcomes for each
particular class was, in Wood's words, "very nearly one of
pure chance."

The senior level examined in 1925 proved to be no better
than the junior in terms of articulation and homogeneity. The
New York regents system, unusually centralized when compared to other states, had utterly failed to produce the standardization that was one of its goals. More than 60 percent of

high school foreign language students were misplaced by at least a semester, with approximately 30 percent of all French students being misplaced by a year or more. The situation was "very near to chaos as far as classification for instructional purposes and as far as educational guidance are concerned."

Wood was not oblivious of the need to measure speaking and listening. For him the best way to measure these was "by means of conversations with students, one at a time, using carefully prepared sets of questions and conversational materials" (1927, 96). Nevertheless, Wood felt that such tests, though valid, would be subjective. He did not include them with his avowedly objective tests. Though Wood had a long subsequent career in testing, he never attempted to produce speaking or listening tests. For several decades thereafter direct oral testing remained alien to the academic environment.

All testers of anything but the simplest construct must make do with a mere sample of the behavior or construct they wish to measure: they cannot hope to cover every single instance and element. Clearly it is the business of the tester to select that sample, based upon a theory, practical experience, pragmatic constraints, or whatever preconceptions he may bring to the task. For this reason all tests are subjective—the claim that the new type tests were objective was false. The objectivity they offered was purely mechanical. The simplified scoring mechanisms that are compatible with an "objective" format were inconsistent with fine discrimination as to quality of response. Of course, even here these tests were not "objective," because the test designer had to decide how much weight to give to each element.

Though now forgotten, the work carried out in New York by Wood and his colleagues remains monumental today, seven decades later. It was a major success for Wood—and an indication of the spirit of inquiry of the times—to have the venerable New York Board of Regents commit its resources to evaluating the claims of the new testing movement, even when they remained unconvinced that the new should supplant the old. The effort needed to administer the tests to tens of thousands of students and the statistical work involved in providing item analyses and measurements of central tendency for all the different tests could only with difficulty be replicated even in today's computer-assisted age. All the tests were hand scored, as it would be some years before machines became available to do this kind of work.

Wood's report was thoughtfully and forcefully argued and came buttressed with an array of statistical charts and tables. If he erred, it was in failing to reflect more profoundly on the problem of how the validity of language tests might be established. At no stage does he appear to have reflected on what it might mean to know a language, and hence how such knowledge might be demonstrated and assessed. Nor did he speculate on the lack of fit between his measuring instruments and the kind of instruction pupils were actually receiving in foreign languages in New York, even though new-type tests were undoubtedly more divorced from contemporary classroom procedures than were the old-type. All his arguments against the current situation were contingent upon his tests being valid, yet he never succeeded in demonstrating the validity of the sample that his tests constituted. It was a common criticism of the new-type tests that they did not tap into what was actually going on in foreign language classrooms, especially at higher levels. If Wood's tests did not properly measure what students were actually being taught in the New York schools, then these tests were no better than the ones they supplanted, and perhaps worse, because the old-type tests for better or worse did reflect many contemporary practices. In the face of doubts such as these, Wood's claims were not accepted uncritically by the Regents Board. An unpublished study purported to show that his findings were invalid (Frizzle 1950, 5), and it was thus long before the regents adopted Wood's innovations.

Wood's tests were based entirely on reading and writing and hence assumed a fairly high level of literacy among those taking them. They inherited much of the format of the Army Alpha tests. The Army Beta tests, designed for use with illiterates or recruits with limited English, do not appear to have attracted any interest among foreign language testers, though from a more modern viewpoint they might have provided an interesting model. The military origin of the testing movement arguably had its effect on the formats adopted during the 1920s, which favored coherence, linear logic, and organization rather than creativity. Generally one and only answer was counted as "right." Like many of his contemporaries, Wood was opposed to translation, feeling that to have students write longhand in any test was a waste of time. The exercise of translation was suspected to have a deleterious effect on students' written English (Woodring 1925). While translation was commonly used as a testing device in the 1920s, the decade saw a decline in its popularity that was never to be reversed in the United States. Translation as a testing procedure remains unpopular even today.

The tests devised by Wood and his colleagues were later published in the form of the Columbia Research Bureau and American Council Alpha and Beta tests. These were widely used and influential for perhaps two decades afterwards. Wood went on to a long and distinguished career in testing, though his association with specifically foreign language testing grew more tenuous in later years. As one of the first to see testing as dependent on techniques and concepts drawn from the scientific method and subject to verification in the real world, Wood deserves to be remembered as the forgotten giant of foreign language testing in America (Downey 1965). In the numbers of students tested Wood's New York experiments have still not been surpassed—a high percentage of high school foreign language students in New York City participated in one or another of Wood's studies. The strong psychometric element in his work has ever since been an important part of the United States language testing tradition.

The Modern Foreign Language Study

Wood's research was but part of an even wider and more ambitious project. Between 1924 and 1927 a massive inquiry into the state of foreign language education was carried out in the United States and Canada. Working with funds provided by the Carnegie Foundation, the U.S. Modern Foreign Language Study (MFLS) Committee and the Canadian Committee on Foreign Languages implemented what even today remains the most comprehensive single survey ever carried out in this field. The initial goals of the committees were to study a wide range of issues including enrollment, achievement, methodology, and teacher training. It was in some aspects an undertaking unique in the history of secondary education. For the first time ever, an effort was made to devise national norms for high schools and colleges, and to statistically compare results achieved by different methods of instruction.

Vivion Henmon's reports (1929a, 1929b) articulated what the most informed and advanced language testers considered to be the issues facing them in the 1920s. According to Henmon (1929b, 3), at least nine separate foreign language skills existed and needed to be tested. These were: vocabulary, reading with comprehension, translation into English, translation into the foreign language, free composition, grammar, auditory comprehension, pronunciation, and speaking. The committee only succeeded in developing tests for four of these: vocabulary, reading, grammar, and composition. A fifth category, listening comprehension, was the subject of research inspired by the study that led to subsequent published tests.

The papers of the study provide an invaluable insight into the state of the art in many areas of foreign language teaching in the mid-1920s. The study produced sixteen standardized foreign language tests, more than all those previously available. Of the sixteen, nine were in French; the rest were divided among German, Spanish, and Italian. The American Council tests were the best known products of the MFLS efforts in testing. An Alpha form of the American Council tests was created for upper high school and college students. Primarily responsible for this test was Vivion Henmon of the University of Wisconsin, who worked in collaboration with Algernon Coleman of the University of Chicago. Part 1 of Henmon's Alpha test (1926) dealt with vocabulary and grammar. Those devising vocabulary tests for the Modern Foreign Language Study were faced with the problem of how to select the words to be tested. A difficult problem at any time, it was made more acute by the many different texts and methodologies used throughout the country, ranging from those with a highly oral and colloquial focus to literary and grammar-translation texts. As Ben Wood put it, "Our textbooks are a veritable Tower of Babel" (1927, 98). Indeed, Wood's comparative word count of sixteen elementary French textbooks had shown that only 134 words were common to all sixteen books. It seemed that in many cases what was being drilled in the classroom was not what was of greatest importance in the language.

For this reason the vocabulary tests devised by the Modern Foreign Language Study were created on the basis of statistics obtained from frequency counts and word lists. As in Wood's New York study, the test was multiple choice. Given five English words, students were asked to mark which one was "a correct translation" of the French word. Two of the distracters were chosen to create "confusion"; two were chosen at random.

> *mais*
>
> hand   more   but   month   day

Henmon defended the rather bare look of these tests on the grounds that "time of administration and cost of printing" were important factors in mass testing of this kind. In answering possible objections to the lack of context of the test items, he offered statistical proof of a high correlation between scores on this type of "column" test and on those tests where words were contextualized. He also testified that while scores on a "recognition" test were consistently higher than on a "recall" test, the correlations were so high that the former, more economical format could safely be used. The recognition test had two advantages; it provided a wider range of sampling and could be easily scored, with somewhat higher scorer reliability than recall. Here were early instances of a theme that runs through the history of foreign language testing, namely, that of the weight that can be legitimately attached to correlations. If Test A correlates highly with scores on Test B, but is much cheaper and easier to run, why replace A with B, regardless of A's patent imperfections?

This issue also emerged in the case of the reading test. In pilot work at the University of Iowa various formats were evaluated, such as foreign language passages with questions in English, passages with questions in the foreign language, true/false answering, and multiple choice. The test designers preferred the paragraphs with multiple-choice format, if only because it was the one most familiar to teachers, but for administrative reasons the study found in favor of the true/false scoring method, in which students had to answer "true" or "false" to a series of statements in English about the foreign language prose reading. The principal rationale offered was that since the true/false answering method was easy to score and yielded scores that correlated highly with other more cumbersome scoring methods there was no reason not to use it. In trying to reduce the memory element in reading tests by working at the sentence level, test designers were missing the importance of paragraph-length discourse in reading. In this decision Henmon perhaps betrayed the influence of his own background. He had no formation in foreign languages, being trained in psychology. He was perhaps too concerned with mechanics and statistics and insufficiently wary of the impoverished use of language called for by true/false responses.

One interesting by-product of the vocabulary test was the discovery that students were often more familiar with words low in the hierarchy of current word lists than with the most common words of French. Thus, the unusual word *ébouriffer* was known to almost as large a percentage of students as the word *ôter*. The conclusion that students were not always learning the most common French vocabulary was supported by the rather low correlations between teachers' marks for vocabulary and students' scores on the vocabulary tests.

The study's grammar tests sought to test "functional grammar" rather than the ability to give paradigms or rules. However, the functional element was still quite weak—the emphasis was on grammar rather than function. The favored elicitation mechanism was completion or selection of equivalent:

> Write the correct form of the article *el, la, lo*.
>
> Estudio _____ lección.

And in German:

> Underscore the correct form:
>
> This is a more expensive chair.
>
> Dies ist ein (mehr, teurer, teuren, teurer, teurerer) Stuhl.

Part 2 of the test dealt with silent reading and composition. Students were issued a picture and told to write "the best composition you can about the picture." Such an unstructured and open-ended task was typical of the time. Though it would seem that the lack of standardization of the writing task must have compromised reliability, in its defense it could be said that it offered a certain validity because of the wide disparity in the level of those who took these tests. Absolute beginners and fluent users of the language alike were free to express themselves according to their ability. The amount of expression called for was in any case extremely limited, because candidates were permitted only the extraordinarily short span of eight minutes in which to write.

The Modern Foreign Language Study took care to address the question of allegedly low interrater reliability for those scoring essay tasks. As early as 1912 Starch and Elliot had conducted a study that seemed to show that grading of English composition could be far from reliable. It was believed that the situation was no better for foreign language composition. The solution adopted by the Modern Foreign Language Study drew on work already carried out in English. Marion Trabue of the University of North Carolina set up a lengthy and quite tortuous process, in which a pilot sample of hundreds of compositions in French was rated by large numbers of judges, and statistical criteria set up. Sixteen compositions were then selected from these to exemplify points on a continuum of excellence. Rather than defining or offering verbal descriptions of discrete levels, a sample for each level was then provided in the form of a particular composition or extract from a composition, with the entire continuum of samples thus constituting the rating scale. Raters had to match the compositions they graded to one of the sixteen points on the continuum. A similar undertaking was carried out for German and Spanish. Breed's (1930) study offered evidence that scoring compositions in this manner yielded higher reliability than when a traditional percentage points mark was assigned to each composition. Generally, reliability was high for all the American Council tests, exceeding .90 in most cases. Intercorrelation between different parts of the tests was high, except that composition scores correlated rather poorly with other elements.

Throughout its work the Modern Foreign Language Study was confronted with the problem of validation. How could test users be sure that the test was doing what it purported to do? What evidence was there that the tests offered valid measurements of student ability? Various attempts were made to confirm this. Scores on tests were correlated with years of study of the foreign language. These correlations turned out to be low, though it could not be determined whether this was because of deficiencies in the tests themselves or because of the invalidity of the criterion. Other criteria, such as correlations with course grades or teachers' marks, were not too high; the best tests in this regard were those for grammar. Intercorrelations between, say, a vocabulary test and a grammar test were fairly but not spectacularly high, generally in the .50

to .60 range. This tended to be offered as evidence for validity, though it also posed the classical dilemma of how to treat the constituent scores yielded by a battery of tests. If tests intercorrelated at high levels, did this mean that they were measuring the same thing? If measuring the same thing, were both really necessary?

The Henmon data were gathered from throughout the United States, taken from tests administered to about five thousand secondary students of French, thirty-three hundred of German, and forty-eight hundred of Spanish. The general findings replicated those of Wood in New York. According to Henmon (1930, 146), "the cumulative evidence is very strong that 50 percent of the students tested are erroneously classified, and should be a semester or more above or below the classifications in which they are found. A similar analysis will show that 25 percent are erroneously classified by a whole year. The situation in the colleges is quite as bad."

Other Tests and Testers

In California Eustace Broom and Walter Kaulfers (1927) devised classroom tests for Spanish reading and vocabulary, normed on thousands of students. One of the formats they recommended was a little more subtle than the current multiple choice. Each item in these exercises consisted of four Spanish words and four English words. Students were told that one of the Spanish words was similar in meaning to one of the English words. They had to say which ones formed a pair. This had the effect of diminishing the influence of guessing. The test was normed on about six thousand pupils.

| sembrar | visita | merengue | profesor |
| rule | teacher | burden | enumerator |

The Modern Foreign Language Study produced few auditory tests. No work in this area appears to have been carried out for German or Italian. M. A. Buchanan of the University of Toronto produced a Spanish audition test for the study. It was originally hoped to put this audition test on phonograph, but this project fell through. Instead, individual teachers were called on to read the script to students. The test consisted of two sets of twenty-five questions. In the first set, the examiner read a one-word stimulus once. Students had to mark the corresponding word from a multiple-choice list, the test calling for students to make a kind of logical association:

agua

beber   nombre   luz   ayer

Twenty-five such stimuli were given, followed by twenty-five more items of a somewhat more complicated nature. The second set likewise followed the principle of answering by association, often creating quite sophisticated tasks. The student had to mark the item most closely associated with the stimulus sentence.

Cuando nos cortamos el dedo sale sangre:

conocimiento   herida   capital   pimiento

Poco a poco se va lejos:

franqueza   eco   paciencia   mirar

The type of language processing required for answering questions such as those in the second set was quite subtle, though to what extent nonlinguistic or cognitive elements entered was moot. The test was very much oriented toward vocabulary, but it was noteworthy for its willingness to mix skills, that is, to have answering dependent on a reading element as well as auditory comprehension. Though the test appears to have been little used, it presented quite an imaginative format. It called for a rather high order of language use, was not based on the single-word level, and made no use of English.

Experimental work on an auditory French test was undertaken by Agnes Rogers in the Philadelphia school system and at Bryn Mawr University. The test was developed too late for the work of the Modern Foreign Language Study, but was published in 1933 as the American Council French Aural Comprehension Test. Though testing one thing at a time had in the 1920s not yet been raised to the status of a theory, even at this early period in the evolution of testing it enjoyed widespread acceptance as desideratum. Thus, in order not to make answering depend on comprehension of written as well as spoken French, the responses to the multiple-choice questions were given in English. The examiner provided the spoken question, and the students marked their answer in English.

> Avec quoi écrit-on?
>
> brush   pen   paper   knife
>
> Quand le soir arrive, qui est fatigué?
>
> worker   idler   owe   night   day

Eighty of these questions were given, in an administration time of thirty-five minutes. The authors were aware of the possible relevance of attention span to success on auditory tests, so no question exceeded the standards set for mother tongue repetition items in the Stanford-Binet test. Contexts were quite impoverished in the Bryn Mawr test, and the vocabulary, drawn as it was from frequency counts of written rather than spoken speech, was not always colloquial. However, Rogers reported satisfactory validation, using teachers' marks as criterion. These were global course marks, rather than marks for the specific listening skill, so the very validation criterion used had itself tested more than one thing at a time and should not therefore have been used for a test that focused on listening comprehension. Parallel-form reliability was around the .80 mark. A serious flaw in reliability arose when the researchers discovered that results differed when students were examined by a native speaker rather than their own teacher (Rogers and Clarke 1933). This interesting weakness was never addressed or remedied.

A more important auditory test, though also produced too late for the work of the study, was the Lundeberg-Tharp Audition-Pronunciation Test in French, initially reported in 1929.

In the first part of the auditory section, on phonetic accuracy, the teacher/examiner read aloud a list that contained fifty sets of similar-sounding words or phrases. The candidate's task was to indicate which of four written versions he had heard:

> Il sait tout
>
> Il s'est tu   Il cède tout   Il se tue   Il sait tout

The phonetic element of this section was quite "pure." Sentences were produced in isolation, allowing no use of context on the part of the listener. The focus was thus entirely on sound rather than meaning. The ability to recognize fairly subtle phonetic distinctions was called upon. Comprehension for meaning was demanded, however, in part 2, in which the tester read a series of twenty incomplete statements in French and students generated the missing words in English.

> S: Le père de ma mère est mon _____
>
> R: grandfather
>
> S: L'eau qui tombe du ciel en gouttes est _____
>
> R: rain

As can be seen, in order for this listening test not to be contaminated by productive ability in French, students were asked to respond in English, regardless of the unnatural blend thus created. However, later versions of the Lundeberg-Tharp test permitted answers for part 2 to be given in French.

The pronunciation section of the Lundeberg-Tharp test contained four parts. In part 1 twenty French words were supplied in writing, each followed by four English words. The English word containing the sound most "similar" to the French was to be marked. In part 2 fifteen French expressions were given, with certain letters in boldface. Pupils were to indicate the English letters that most closely expressed the sounds of the letters in boldface. Part 3 required the indication of the silent letters in twenty French words. In part 4 twenty word groups were listed, with the student having to determine whether liaison should be made. The entire test was thus given in written form, with no oral or auditory component.

Tharp, who was a professor of French at Ohio State University, saw this format as valid, as it attempted "to measure the mental equipment of an individual which would enable him to pronounce French correctly, with the hope that a close correlation could be shown between this and actual speech" (Tharp 1931, 4). No evidence for this "close correlation" was supplied.

The Lundeberg-Tharp test was standardized on fifteen hundred high school and college students and yielded satisfactory reliability figures. The reliability for the audition test was 0.85; that for pronunciation was a little lower. Correlations with scores on other tests, such as dictation or pronunciation tests, were relatively high: 0.53 between Tharp's pronunciation test and Greenleaf's test and 0.77 between the audition test and a dictation test (Tharp 1931). The entire Lundeberg-Tharp test took about thirty minutes to administer. It had a long working life, outlasting all the other tests of the 1920s.

Tharp's test was not the first effort to tackle the hitherto insoluble problem of testing spoken speech. Aurelio Espinosa reported work in developing an oral part to the Stanford Spanish test (1927), but the researchers appear to have lost heart in the face of the obvious difficulties of creating such a test. Though the Stanford test did appear and indeed was for many years widely used, it did not contain the projected section on pronunciation.

More concrete work in French came in the form of Jeanne Greenleaf's French pronunciation test (1929), which is especially interesting for the fact that it made use of the technology of the Dictaphone. The student made a recording of his speech by reading a short passage of French into the Dictaphone. This was subsequently scored for pronunciation. Greenleaf was vague on how this scoring was carried out. She did, however, report that the average time of administration was two minutes, and that she had to administer and grade about four hundred such tests unaided every semester. Scores

on Greenleaf's test correlated with those on the oral section
of the Lundeberg-Tharp test at the level of .53. Greenleaf's un-
timely death put a stop to her work, however, and her test per-
ished with her. Greenleaf's test was characteristic of the time
in isolating an element such as pronunciation from its
function within the entire expression. Speech, at least in its
manifestation for testing, was seen as reading aloud or
uttering one-way discourse. It was not seen as interactive, and
the sole focus for grading tended to be pronunciation.

Nevertheless, to appreciate the comparative modernity of
Greenleaf's test it is only necessary to contrast it with other
methods of testing pronunciation. As late as the mid-1920s
the New York Regents examination offered written pronunciation tests such as:

> Indicate the main difficulty or peculiarity in the sound of one
> consonant in each of the following words or phrases:
>
> absurde, soixante, nom anglais, cent un, grand homme

An auditory element was introduced in the 1927 Regents
exam in French. This consisted of a dictation and a content
comprehension test. In the latter the teacher asked oral questions about a passage he had read to the class. Students wrote
their answers. This replaced the "credit for oral work" grade, a
mark impressionistically assigned by teachers to their own
students, which appears to have been somewhat abused. Simultaneously, the "phonetics" section was dropped. These
moves were designed to reward true oral work in the classroom. The dictation and the passage for aural comprehension
were read twice, and instructors were provided with marked
breath groups to tell them how to divide the passages for reading. The readings were "at about the speed of the usual public
speaker." Grading was based on deducting for errors, with
each word counting as one unit. All errors were to be
counted "without distinction or differentiation." This included "accents, capitalization, punctuation and division of
syllables at end of lines." In the content comprehension test,

more credit was given for evidence of comprehension than for quality of expression in French.

Stimulated by the environment of inquiry fostered by the Modern Foreign Language Study, tests began to appear with "somewhat bewildering frequency" (Welch and Van Horne 1928, 615). The famous De Sauzé devised his own tests as part of his work in Cleveland. Surprisingly, they do not show the communicative emphasis De Sauzé argued for in his work with teachers, but are similar to other new-type tests, with a high reliance on partial translation. A large number of books and articles appeared on how to apply the methodology of the "new tests" to daily classroom use. For the first time ever, the topic of testing was assigned a prime place in the agenda of meetings of professional organizations. A talk on modern language testing at a conference of high school teachers at the University of Illinois in November 1926 "provoked enthusiasm and discussion" (*Modern Language Journal*, January 1927, 238). Two years later, in November 1928, an entire session on testing was held at the meeting of the Illinois conference; one of the concrete outcomes was the Lundeberg-Tharp test mentioned earlier. The American Association of Teachers of French (AATF) annual meeting of 1927 offered a session titled "How shall we measure achievement in modern languages?", probably the first such session held anywhere. There was even a nationwide contest in 1929 in which participants constructed tests for French and Spanish.

These were the years of the founding of important professional organizations, such as the American Association for the Teaching of German and the American Association for the Teaching of French, the first Summer Linguistics Institute (1928), the inception of the Scholastic Aptitude Test (1926), the appearance of such journals as the *French Review* (1928) and the *German Quarterly* (1928), and the reappearance of the German-language teaching *Monatshefte* after their closure during the First World War.

An atmosphere of optimism and dynamism prevailed in regard to the possibilities of a new "scientific" basis for foreign language teaching and testing. Researchers were anxious to come to grips with the diverse questions facing foreign language teachers, and, for a few years at least, many were confident that the new tests provided by the Modern Foreign Language Study would furnish an important tool for this purpose. In Henmon's words, they were opening up "a field that would be carried on further." Some universities began to switch to new-type testing. The University of Wisconsin was one of the strongholds of the new wave. In 1930 a large study comparing new-style and old-style testing was carried out at that university. It found in favor of the new tests on grounds of reliability, because standards of rating old-style examinations varied widely. Tests at the University of Wisconsin were used for placement and to avoid students' repeating levels of instruction that they did not need. Students were able to have the foreign language requirement waived by passing a "proficiency" examination largely composed of multiple-choice translation and completion exercises and a structured essay.

However great the numbers of studies, however wide their sweep, the fact is that the greater part of testing was and is done in semiprivate, by class teachers. Many years later Ben Wood (1956, 58) wryly reminisced of the 1920s testing movement: "The schoolmen who were the bulk of our audiences quite frankly admitted they did not understand the technical lingo, and only politeness led them to conceal their suspicion that the technicians didn't either." It would be prudent to presume considerable resistance to the new-type tests at this level. Fife (1931, 99) wrote of the "formidable" opposition that the tests had met:

> The unfamiliar character of the new forms, an unwillingness to accept the validity of the mathematical reasoning on which general conclusions from tests administrations are based, and especially the traditional feeling that an examination in order to bring reliable results must be made to correspond to teaching practices and must furnish a model for future teaching practice, are some of the causes which have prevented a

> wider acceptance of the new-type tests and will, no doubt, continue to render their progress difficult among more conservative teachers.

However, in general Fife held that the reception of the new-type tests by teachers had been "quite enthusiastic." Bagster-Collins (1930, 96), one of the few writers to evince skepticism about the new tests, worried about their undesirable backwash effect in the classroom: "The true and false statements used in the present tests err on the side of being stupid, and to many they are obnoxious." One pair of bibliographers was less than effusive in recording the plethora of "objective (perhaps one might even say mechanistic) measurement" (Welch and Van Horne 1928, 617). Spiers (1927) translated paragraphs from a French new-type test into English. When his students at Columbia University took the test in English, they achieved an average score of only 83 percent. Spiers argued that nonlinguistic factors had too large a place in the new tests. Louis Mercier, president of the American Association of Teachers of French, offered a critique that would be relevant to testing debates in a later time and context: "As, in the effort to standardize tests, we are reduced to test only one item at a time, we may be permitted to doubt whether through such tests we can ever get at the composite linguistic development status of our pupils." Multiple-choice tests, for Mercier, were "purely passive and offer no criterion of dynamic knowledge" (1933, 382). Completion tests, in his view, gave "no proof that the item could function as the stimulus of an idea." As might be expected, it was not only foreign language teachers who were unpersuaded by the new testing formats; teachers in general were reluctant to accept the claims of standardized testing at face value (Raftery 1988). The College Board examinations persisted as purely reading and writing, with particular value being attached to translation into English. In one writer's phrase (Robert 1927), in these exams French was treated as "a dead language."

One of the striking aspects of the foreign language testing boom of the 1920s is its divorce from linguistics. Linguistics at this time still saw its function as philological inquiry rather than speculation on the nature of language and how it is acquired or learned. While the 1920s saw a certain groping for a theory of testing, there was no exposition of the importance of a theory of language. Stephen Gould's remarks (1981, 263) on Spearman are apposite, if a little harsh in the foreign language context: "He [Spearman] had contempt for the atheoretical empiricism of the testers, their tendency to construct tests by throwing apparently unrelated items together and then offering no justification for such a curious procedure beyond the claim that it yielded good results." Language testing and theories of language stayed on separate tracks for many years after the 1920s, even after linguistics had defined its role as a research discipline more clearly.

Precisely for the reasons described earlier, the 1920s witnessed something of a boom in "prognosis testing"—what today would be called aptitude testing. The underlying goal of the broad testing movement was the creation of a society where everyone would do what he was best able to do. Binet (quoted in Gumbert and Spring 1974, 88) wrote of a future "where everyone would work according to his known aptitudes in such a way that no particle of psychic force should be lost for society." The need for some kind of predictive testing seemed especially pressing given the large numbers of students now entering the educational process. Some argued that the influx of large numbers was damaging the prospects of the best students. Barlow (1926, 32), the president of the American Association of Teachers of Spanish (AATS), told his organization that

> we have in the early terms in high school a horde of low IQs. These low IQs get into our modern language classes together with their more gifted brethren. The pace has to be set for the latter. The weak ones cannot keep step, and they swell the percentage of failure at the end of the term, after having received attention that could more profitably have been given to their brighter comrades.

Barlow approvingly noted the efforts made in New York in the early 1920s to permit only the brightest pupils to take foreign language in high school. George Rice (1930) of the University of California visited 22 modern language classes in California in 1925-26. He saw no evidence of any attempt by teachers to cater to individual ability differences among their students—what he called "elasticity." He further surveyed students to see how long they spent in foreign language home study. Generally the better students spent less time on study than the weaker ones. Rice argued that schools were failing in their duty to the brighter students in not demanding more of them. "With the ever-increasing inclusion in our high school population of students of inferior linguistic ability, the average capacity and average achievement is being continually lowered and the superior pupil is getting less education." Rice called for more grouping by ability level and greater use of prognosis tests. Where these were not possible, he urged greater "elasticity" in teaching that would require more from the bright students and not give the weak a sense of failure.

Coleman (1929) echoed this: "It would also be highly advantageous both to pupils and to effective teaching in modern languages if school authorities would cooperate in grouping students on the basis of their previous scholastic record and of scores on intelligence tests, and if they would make it possible to reclassify or drop from the subject those who do not keep up with their classes, whether from incapacity or from other causes."

In this climate many educators and administrators looked for ways of putting order on the incipient chaos in foreign language education by removing from the process those who would never make much progress in it. Li's doctoral dissertation at Harvard University (1927) was probably the first dissertation devoted to any problem of foreign language placement. Li was interested in the relationship between measured intelligence and success in language learning. He found that scores on intelligence tests correlated quite low with scores on the American Council tests in French. He reasoned that this tended to show that other factors were at work in determining student success.

As has been seen, a number of writers recommended weeding out deficient students by examining their IQ scores and their scores in English. Some teachers instituted trial periods from two weeks to a year to select those who would benefit and cull those who would not benefit from further language study. More formal prognosis tests were published (Henmon 1929). One, the Barry Prognosis Test, used a little Spanish, on the theory that to find out how well a student will do in Spanish, one should see how well he does on some Spanish. Barry claimed to have calculated correlations of around .60 between scores on his test and teachers' marks in a subsequent Spanish course. Other commonly used early tests were the Iowa Foreign Language Placement Test, the Symonds Prognosis Test, the Luria-Orleans Test, the Wilkins Test, and the George Washington University Test.

Stoddard and Vander Beke (1925) designed the Iowa Placement Test. They showed that a fair relationship existed between this battery and first-semester grades at the University of Iowa. James Tharp, who continued work with the Iowa test, determined a 50 percent predictive value for this when measured against first-semester grades. Percival Symonds of Columbia's Teachers College used the Iowa test as part of a more complex battery, reporting a correlation around .60 with objective examinations in foreign language after a period of study. All of these tests were oriented toward academic success in the language, so they tended to focus on testing ability to put grammatical rules into practice in particular exercises, as well as on translating to/from the specimen language.

None of the 1920s tests sought to measure a person's ability to discriminate foreign language sounds. Hence they were quite like verbal intelligence tests, since they focused on the ability to decipher written texts. Word-based rather than discourse-based, they were oriented toward the most academically inclined students. They were used not so much to see which students had an aptitude for foreign languages but rather which students did not. A later reviewer wrote: "Foreign language prognosis tests of the Symonds and Luria-Orleans type are usually excellent means for reducing foreign language enrollments in nonfunctional courses taught by teachers incapable of adjusting either method or content to the needs, interests and abilities of children" (Kaulfers 1940, 1341).

William Barlow (1926, 33), the AATS president, was especially shrewd in noticing a weakness of aptitude testing that has often gone undetected. He pointed out that a prognosis test provided no basis for predicting if a particular student would profit from foreign language study. In fact, one could not speak about someone benefiting from foreign language study unless one could define the benefits of foreign language study.

> The vast majority leave school with little book knowledge, and soon lose what they have. These people have, however, grown in various ways, and have developed certain attitudes of mind . . . a prognosis test which does not take them into account, but merely indicates that one pupil is apt to be slower than another in his progress in language study is not satisfactory.

Regrettably, Barlow's remarks failed to open up a debate on the goals and purposes of foreign language learning. Seven decades later language testers have yet to address the questions of why people should study foreign languages and how we can judge whether that study has benefited them beyond specific linguistic outcomes.

In sum, the 1920s were the decade of the great boom in foreign language testing in the United States. An astonishing number of tests were devised and published; by the close of the decade there were probably as many as fifty tests published for foreign languages. Whatever the weaknesses of these tests were on the level of the individual student, on the mass level the studies provided a more comprehensive picture of achievement than has ever subsequently been available. A small corps of people emerged who saw themselves as professional language testers, and a very lively intellectual interchange sprang up between them. While not always in agreement about how to devise tests, the leading figures in the field found a common basis for deciding how tests themselves must be tested and proved. Though foreign language testers have probably always been aware—if only subconsciously—of such issues as reliability and validity, in the 1920s these terms were thought of for the first time as being best established by experiment and statistics rather than through intuition or experience. The decade witnessed the breakdown of the influence of the old test format, which had been rooted in the teaching and testing of the classical languages and in which metalinguistic knowledge occupied a central role. This was replaced by tests that sought to measure "functional" knowledge of the language.

This "functional" knowledge, however, was a long way from what would be understood by the term today. Using "objective" formats such as multiple choice and matching, tests focused on vocabulary and grammar, measured in short, contextless segments. Little attention was paid to composition or other writing skills such as paraphrase or translation. There was very little auditory, and almost no oral testing. Vocabulary was chosen "scientifically," but few recognized the limitations of word counts. For instance, in a word count the days of the week might appear quite low in the hierarchy, suggesting that this was not something a student needed to learn early. In the absence of broad goals for language learning, particular tests seemed to be designed for their own sake, not integrated into an overall program. And the statistical methods employed were quite rudimentary by today's standards—there was no realization, for example, of the effects of probable error.

However, despite these and other deficiencies, the 1920s in many ways stand as a high point in the history of foreign language testing. At no subsequent time have so many figures from leading universities—many of them departmental chairmen—so enthusiastically committed themselves to language teaching and testing. Robert Fife, for instance, was chair of the Department of German at Columbia College. Could a similar phenomenon take place today? How often do chairs of language departments at Ivy League universities get involved in language teaching controversies? As Eddy (1930) wrote of the great foreign language studies of the latter half of the 1920s: "In no other subject at the secondary level has a comparable body of data been assembled, critically studied and made available to the public." It would be several decades before testing would witness anything like the same excitement and enthusiasm, and the scale of the research of the 1920s still remains to be equaled.

Much of the effort in the 1920s was expended on devising measures that would furnish scores that were comparable between schools and across semesters. The Modern Foreign Language Study's great interest in testing was actually a by-product of its original goals. The study's primary objectives were to gain data about achievement in foreign language and to find out what helped or hindered it. It never truly got to the point of addressing this question, since it was from the beginning faced with the problem of how to measure the outcomes it wished to study. The various tests devised were seen as constituting only the first phase of the study, and as being no more than the required tools for carrying forward the real object of the investigation. Though devising measures that would be comparable between schools and across semesters was only to be the means to an end, the study spent so much time on testing that it never reached its end. The Modern Foreign Language Study experience thus showed the utter centrality of testing to educational research. It provided a lesson that later generations rarely heeded: goals are not abstract; they must be concretely set within an educational context and a time frame. Now, seven decades later, comparability of achievement between one school and another or one university and another is not much higher than it was at the time of the Modern Foreign Language Study.

Those participating in the Modern Foreign Language Study were not unwilling to gather data in the population as a whole by going out into the classrooms. They tried out their tests on large and unwieldy numbers of subjects. In this they still stand as an example to some of today's testers. The foreign language measurement instruments of the 1920s may not be very good in our eyes, but that should not blind us to the achievements of those who devised them. For the first time, those involved in teaching foreign languages were consciously reflecting on the question of how to assess learning outcomes and, in doing so, were creating the very idea of testing as a discrete activity. Seeking to found their discipline on a scientific methodology, they incorporated all the then available tools of statistics and technology. For decades the work of the Modern Foreign Language Study stood as state of the art in language testing. As late as 1948 Newmark would write in his preface (ix) that "the Modern Foreign Language Study is still exemplary of the best that we have accomplished as a profession." One sees references to the Modern Foreign Language Study in the pedagogical literature well into the 1940s and even 1950s.

As it turned out, however, not much came directly of the great language-testing boom of the 1920s. The efforts to reform foreign language teaching and testing in the 1920s largely failed. Leaving aside social and economic factors in the wider world, the great weakness of the testing pioneers of the 1920s lay in their failure to reflect on how to establish the validity of language tests. They never noticed the lack of fit between the new measurement instruments and the kind of instruction pupils were actually receiving in foreign languages. Nor did they seek to develop any theory or construct of language that might have provided some coherence or logic in deciding which elements to test and how to test them. There is very little questioning of the nature of language in the 1920s and not much debate about what it is that is being tested. There is little evidence that testing researchers had an appreciation for the complexity of the task of learning a second language. Though it was in the 1920s that linguistics developed as an academic profession (Hymes and Fought 1975), language teachers and testers worked in isolation from linguistics. It is doubtful, however, that linguistics as practiced at the time was in a position to supply a theory of language to justify particular testing formats. While the researchers of the 1920s deserve praise for their willingness to work in the field with large numbers of subjects, their failure showed that mere use of large populations in testing research is not enough.

3

The Depression Decade

As the decade of the 1920s ended, United States education entered a period of significant change. Almost 50 percent of universities had no language requirement for admission. Within the secondary schools the number of electives was growing, with new curricular options jostling out foreign languages. Foreign language enrollment began to decline in percentage terms. The demand for a patently utilitarian education became insistent, and foreign language was not deemed to fall under this rubric (Rippa 1964). Rather than being seen as an essential part of the core curriculum for high school, foreign language began to be lumped with subjects such as art or music—very laudable pursuits, undoubtedly, but thought best restricted to the minority of children who possessed an aptitude for them. Even the New York Regents, for so long strong supporters of foreign language, ruled in 1935 that a foreign language was no longer required for a Regents diploma. A few years later a survey of foreign language teachers in New York showed that a majority favored the abolition of the Regents language examination itself (Frizzle 1950, 6). Throughout the country curriculum planners sought to introduce a new emphasis on teaching for citizenship and for inculcating an awareness of social problems, and the U.S. curriculum began to turn inward on itself (Handschin 1940, 19-20; Huebener 1944, 168-70). New foreign language curricula were drawn up that "sought to stress the interrelationship between the American and the foreign civilization" (Frizzle 1950, 17)—courses oriented toward culture rather than language.

The general climate of the time was thus not propitious for expansion in foreign language pedagogical research. Specifically, little of the pioneering work of the 1920s matured in the subsequent decade. Rather than acquiring new vigor from the publication of the results of the Modern Foreign Language Study, the research impetus lost strength. Undoubtedly, one factor in this was the economic depression. A contributor to the *French Review* in 1933 wrote ruefully of the catastrophe of the great slump. Twenty-five thousand teachers had lost their jobs, though a million more pupils had come into the schools. Many school boards had gone broke, defaulting on bonds, closing schools and firing teachers, shortening instruction time, even charging for tuition where before it had been free (Kurz 1934).

Those who created the standardized tests put out as part of the Modern Foreign Language Study had hoped that they would be of great utility to a wide range of researchers in subsequent years. In reality, rather than continuing to expand in the 1930s, the research bubble burst, and little was done to push forward the laboriously created achievements of the Modern Foreign Language Study. Indeed the 1930s brought general disenchantment with standardized testing. Carl Brigham charged the commercial testers with being more interested in selling tests than in improving them, and with lacking the broad cultural background appropriate to the tester: "Testers having chosen their own weapon and set up their own target then told educators that this was the right one to shoot at" (Brigham 1937, 758).

Though the environment for foreign language research was no longer supportive, another factor in the foreign language slump of the 1930s was the outcome of the Modern Foreign Language Study itself. Algernon Coleman's report in 1929, *The Teaching of Modern Foreign Languages in the United States*, was only one of seventeen volumes produced by the study and indeed had appeared rather late in the series, as volume twelve of seventeen. Nevertheless, Coleman's report came to stand in the eyes of much of the profession for the considered results of the entire work of the study. Coleman's treatise was quite a complex and less than dogmatic document, but its primary recommendation was to set reading as the primary goal of the two-year language sequence. This was a somewhat ironic development, because just a couple of decades earlier the MLA Committee of Twelve of 1898 had put reading at the bottom of its list of goals. In putting forward the teaching of reading as the central aspiration of foreign language education, Coleman based himself on grounds not so much theoretical as practical. His recommendation was essentially rooted in two of the major findings of the Modern Foreign Language Study. In the first place, it had been shown that many students received only one year of foreign language study, and that very few received more than two. Second, a survey of the language teaching force had found it wanting in many areas of preparation, especially in the spoken foreign language.

What goals, then, could be realistically achieved within the given constraints of time, resources, and personnel? Rather than attempt to teach all four skills, speaking, listening, reading, and writing, and succeed in none, Coleman reasoned that deliberate concentration on one of them might yield worthwhile results. The one with the greatest short-term yield, or "surrender value" as it was often called, appeared to be reading. To a large extent there was little that was revolutionary about Coleman's recommendation, because, despite the MLA committee's prescription, reading had in any case always been a central goal in the teaching of foreign languages in the United States, at any rate at the university level. Coleman merely canonized what was already a widespread practice. The second of the ten goals listed by Coleman—unnoticed in the general hubbub about reading—was teaching "the ability to communicate orally with the natives." Coleman advocated transfer of the emphasis not from an oral concentration to reading, but rather from grammar to reading. This point was lost in the controversy, and the enthronement of the reading goal came to be forever seen as the only recommendation of the Coleman report.

Many of the people associated with the Modern Foreign Language Study were attached to universities rather than high schools. To some extent this could have contributed to the bookish bent of their findings. The concept of reading espoused by Coleman and his supporters was quite a narrow one. Material to be read was predominantly literary, and the report showed little awareness of the wide register of reading materials that would today be considered fit subjects for work in the foreign language classroom. The daily reality of the reading method was even less ambitious than its stated objectives, because in many schools instead of the prescribed texts sets of summaries and notes on those texts were read. Years later Arthur Bovée (1949, 384) suggested that what went on in the reading-based class was not in fact reading but "puzzled decipherment."

The validity of Coleman's supposed preference for reading was challenged by others in the profession, who countered by pointing to the increased opportunities for oral and auditory practice opened up by such phenomena as popular access to foreign travel, the talking cinema, phonograph, and radio. Several prominent members of the Committee of Investigation of the Modern Foreign Language Study disassociated themselves from Coleman's report, and a formal rebuttal of Coleman was signed by some eighty professors and teachers and published (French Review 1931, 386-96). The effect of the whole controversy was to spoil the many worthwhile fruits of the study. Henceforth little attention was paid to the results of its laborious and costly research. Indeed, it seemed that the perceived outcome of the Modern Foreign Language Study served only to diminish the stature of foreign language research.

Though the 1930s were thus a time of limited innovation in language teaching, some use was made of the tests produced in the previous decade. Stevenson (1934) reported that placement at the University of Pittsburgh was effected by using various standardized tests. Miner (1931) used the Stanford Spanish tests to compare high-school and college achievement. Clarke (1931) administered the Bryn Mawr listening test to New York high school students. The University of North Carolina adopted the American Council tests as part of its placement program (Giduz 1937). These or other standardized tests were used in several universities to divide students into sections on the basis of ability (Seibert and Goddard 1934).

The creation of new standardized language tests slowed somewhat, though one exception to this trend was provided by the Cooperative Test Service, set up by the American Council on Education in 1930. As the name implied, the Cooperative Test Service aspired to fostering greater cooperation in the preparation of tests than had hitherto been the norm. Instead of tests being identified with one or two people, as had been the case with some tests in the 1920s, the participation of experts throughout the country was enlisted. The Cooperative tests were not universally admired. Nelson Brooks in the *First Mental Measurements Yearbook* (1938) wrote of these tests:

> A test of this sort, in attempting to give a cross-section picture of achievement in language, can at best afford only an oblique and partial view. Many a student will find himself dealing with problems that are artificial in the extreme, as they are quite foreign to French and are not likely to occur to the student's mind. (Buros 1938, 81)

In the succeeding *Mental Measurements Yearbook*, Joseph Jackson wrote of the Cooperative tests in words that presaged later debates about the nature of language proficiency:

> If there are important aspects of language study which cannot be scientifically tested and objectively measured, does the objective test furnish an adequate description of the student's general ability? (Buros 1940, 171)

The Cooperative foreign language tests consisted of a reading section, a vocabulary section, and a grammar section.

They tended to be all constructed after the same plan, using formats such as multiple choice and completion. They avoided translation passages and emphasized what was claimed to be functional knowledge rather than metalinguistic. These tests were to remain popular for a considerable time. A decade after they were first published, they were still of sufficient relevance for Prescott Smith in 1942 to report data on the validity of the Cooperative French Test. A number of universities made use of forms of the Cooperative tests until well into the 1970s and as late as the 1980s. Columbia University in New York was using the Cooperative Foreign Language (Spanish) Tests in placing incoming freshmen. The Cooperative Testing Service designed the new-look achievement tests that were initially adopted by the College Board on an experimental basis in 1937. The service was to be subsumed within the Educational Testing Service (ETS) when the latter was instituted in 1948.

Ben Wood, an important figure in setting up the Cooperative Testing Service, continued his contributions to testing through his work on the creation of a machine for scoring tests. In 1928 Wood was made a consultant to IBM, which was already seeking to design a test-scoring machine. Because of practical difficulties, such as the inability of the machines to deal with differing shades of darkness in pencil marks, it was several years before the problem was solved. In 1935 the IBM model 805 finally came on the market, the first commercial test-scoring machine (Traxler 1953). The development of such machines permitted a massive expansion in testing all subjects, at greatly decreased costs. In the case of foreign language, the introduction of machine scoring merely confirmed the already existing trend toward multiple choice, the focus on recognition questions rather than production, and the neglect to test such things as autonomous writing or speech. It would be years later before anyone questioned whether the effects of widespread "objective" testing were totally benign.

The movement toward "objective" testing in foreign language was very strong at the University of Wisconsin, where such tests were used for placement and to prevent students from repeating levels of instruction that they did not need. Students were able to have the foreign language requirement waived by passing a "proficiency" examination, largely composed of multiple-choice translation and completion exercises and a structured essay. There was an oral examination also; the criterion was that the student should show such speaking knowledge as might be expected of a student after one year's study (Cheydleur 1931). The French test at Wisconsin was validated against scores on the Columbia Research Bureau French test, yielding a correlation of .75.

While the Wisconsin test was not a particularly interesting example of the craft of test design, it was notable for the fact that by using it a major university accepted the new-type testing formats. It was quite novel for a university to use an achievement test in foreign languages instead of its traditional class-based tests. It was also a rarity to see economic issues so explicitly linked to questions of testing. In the light of the general poverty caused by the Depression, the authorities at the University of Wisconsin were very proud of the fact that their students could save money by scoring well on achievement tests and would thus have to take few or no language courses. Placement was seen in financial terms; appropriate placement of students excused them from taking unnecessary courses and so saved money, both for the individual and for the community at large. The notion of accurate placement as a social duty is one that shows the spirit of the 1930s but is subsequently rarely seen in foreign language testing. Frederic Cheydleur, who ran the French program at Wisconsin, calculated that many thousands of dollars were saved yearly by the University's placement program.

The testing of written compositions had to some extent been neglected in the tests developed in the 1920s. Because work on rater reliability in the evaluation of written English composition had seemed to show great disparities in standards, several of the most prominent foreign language testers avoided composition altogether. One exception to this was research carried out within the Modern Foreign Language Study, which led to the creation of composition grading scales following Hillegas and Trabue's work with English, in which sample compositions exemplified points on a continuum of merit. Seibert and Goddard (1934) reported, however, that these grading scales were in practice of limited use, often failing to assign particular compositions to a unique point on the scale. As an innovation, Seibert and Goddard used a story rather than a picture to elicit writing. Students heard a story in English and then had to retell it in written French. Grading was carried out through a rather complex system, based on the criterion of density of errors per one hundred words. The researchers reported high correlations between scores on this test and teachers' estimates of writing ability.

Some other research published in the 1930s exemplified an effort to build on the foundation provided by the Modern Foreign Language Study. Feder and Cochran (1936) devised a variation of the multiple-choice format. Instead of having students select one correct option out of four, they had to mark which was the best answer and which was the worst. The four options had been set up so as to embody gradations in correctness. One was right, one was wrong, the other two were partially correct. The authors reported a correlation of around .50 with scores on other tests of reading. This was an interesting development of the stark multiple-choice format, offering a subtlety and cognitive dimension otherwise often lacking. The rather low correlations it yielded with other measures perhaps betrayed the possibility that nonlinguistic factors such as intelligence were at play.

A logical development of new-type testing in language was to apply it to testing literature. One effort to marry the new-type tests to the examination of literature used completions, matchings, and fill-in-the-blanks (Alpern 1933). Examinees, in this case candidates for jobs as Spanish teachers, had to answer multiple-choice questions such as:

The first important literary genre to develop in Spain was

a) the novel   *b)* the drama   *c)* epic poetry   *d)* the pastoral
romance   *e)* biography

Another series of questions used the completion technique:

Menéndez y Pelayo rates the three most important works of
Spanish literature as

_____ _____ _____ .

Alpern believed that the test offered all the advantages of
the new-type testing: ease of grading, objectivity, accuracy,
possibility of quickly testing large numbers, etc. Given the
extensive or "outside" reading advocated by Coleman and
many other theorists, amounting to the coverage of hundreds,
if not thousands, of pages, the question arose of how to monitor and test this. Seibert and Goddard (1931) recommended a
true/false format, suggesting that an average book-length reading might warrant as many as one hundred true/false. In urging that the true/false statements should be unequivocally true
or false, they left no room for nuance or interpretation, which
many might have seen as one of the benefits of extensive reading. At Columbia University students of French were given
twenty-four hours to read an assigned French book. At the
end of the twenty-four hours they had to write a 750-word ré-
sumé of the book and a 250-word evaluation, both in English
(Sammartino 1938).

Kaulfers (1933) reported on "a citation test" of extensive
reading. This was an open-book test in which students had to
point out where certain facts were to be found in a long passage they had been assigned to read. The questions, given in
English, were on the order of "Who said what?" and "What
was so-and-so's job?" Candidates wrote down the page and
line number of where the information could be located in the
text. In 1940 Geiger described tests of outside reading that
included even more specific information. Candidates were
asked to supply such things as the name of the publisher,
whether the book contained an introduction or illustrations,

and whether the chapters had titles. Cases such as these suggest that the marriage between the reading goal and contemporary testing practices was an unhappy one. Despite a good deal of interest in the topic, no rational body of testing ever evolved to match the particular needs and goals of the reading method.

The College Boards generally lost influence during the 1930s, especially when the egalitarian New Deal atmosphere made selectivity a less desirable trait than it had been earlier. Between 1926 and 1935 the number of students taking College Board tests almost halved, from twenty-two thousand to fewer than fourteen thousand (Valentine 1987, 39). However, the Scholastic Aptitude Test began to be a lucrative source of income for the boards. Developments in the boards examinations at this time were slow but real. A commission appointed to update the boards' requirements reported in 1932, urging that some concessions be made to the new-type testing methods. It was not till 1934 that limited action was taken to introduce elements of the new-type tests in the College Board French examination.

The new examination contained five sections:

1. Reading comprehension

2. Objective grammar test (completions and partial translation)

3. French to English translation

4. English to French translation

5. Free composition

This structure represented a rather heavy weight for translation. The College Board had publicly accepted the validity of the reading goal, yet it was noticeable to how small a degree the new format corresponded to that goal. In 1934 scoring keys were furnished to graders of the College Board examinations, leading to somewhat higher rater reliability (Tharp 1940). Despite these efforts to increase the reliability of the examinations, there was still a lot of variation between languages. In any given year the French examination might or might not be much harder than the Spanish. Generally, the format remained conservative. French examinations tended to stress vocabulary and grammar, with a little pronunciation. German examinations stressed translation and grammar. New-type questions were used most commonly in the Spanish examinations. (This tendency for German to stress form and specifics and for French to be broader and more integrative can be discerned many times and at different levels in the history of foreign language testing.) At least the lack of oral or auditory elements was logical, because reading ability and grammatical knowledge were what students would be expected to show once they got to college.

The College Board introduced achievement tests in 1937. These tests were initially supplied by Wood's Cooperative Testing Service and were adopted with a view to attracting students from outside the traditional catchment areas of the Ivy League schools. The tests were not bound to any curriculum and used multiple-choice rather than essay formats. The new examination was shorter—one hour, as opposed to the previous three hours—and was now administered four times a year. In 1942 the achievement tests totally supplanted the old-fashioned College Board examinations in existence since the beginning of the century. The new Achievement Tests represented a considerable break with tradition. The old College Board examinations had been instituted in order to make preparatory schools conform to the curricular and admission standards of the universities. The achievement tests, on the other hand, represented a disavowal of any influence on the part of the College Board. "Instead of using the tests to determine curricula, the curricula as they existed would determine the content of the tests" (Dyer 1964, 7).

In 1930 the College Board constructed a test with a view to helping American universities judge the proficiency in English of foreign students who came to pursue their studies in the United States. The test consisted of four parts. The first was reading comprehension, in which candidates read English passages and answered true/false questions. The second part was listening comprehension, consisting of two dictated passages. The first passage was to be transcribed verbatim, while the second was used as basis for an original composition by the candidate. The third part was a written composition—a minimum of 250 words to be written within an hour and a half—while the final part was an oral interview of ten to fifteen minutes. It appears that a version of this test had already been in use in the 1920s. In 1932 the College Board sought to find out at which level their English exam might be used in the universities. Of 125 universities and colleges that responded to the board's question, fewer than 20 promised to require their incoming foreign students to take the examination (College Board 1932; Spolsky 1993). This lack of interest persisted in subsequent years.

The New York Regents examination evolved throughout the decade at a somewhat faster pace. In 1930 the composition question was removed from the second-year Regents examination. Two new questions were added, one on civilization and one in which students answered spoken questions. In the latter auditory section the examiner read an anecdote twice, then read five questions based on it. The students wrote their answers in the foreign language. The translation passage tended to be quite long—perhaps as many as twenty lines to be translated into English. For a long time the reading section on the Regents exam was worth much less than the translation element. This drew from those who favored the reading method the criticism that the examination failed to adapt to the new climate. In 1937 the importance of translation was diminished, and increased significance was attached to reading comprehension.

The Modern Foreign Language Study's tests escaped the main controversy occasioned by the Coleman report, though Coleman was very dissatisfied with the quality of tests in everyday use. While public attacks on "objective" and standardized testing of foreign languages were few, the long-

standing old-style tradition continued to have many supporters. It is prudent to presume that there was a large gap
between what appeared in the professional literature and what
actually transpired in classrooms. A report on the progress of
the New York Teachers Examination for Oral Credit showed
that this examination had remained quite immune from the
new-type testing methodology (Price 1933). The exam consisted of four parts:

1. Translate a French passage to English. In addition, write in
   phonetic script the pronunciation of certain words used in
   the passage.

2. Define in French 20 words taken from text.

3. Translate to French 19 idiomatic phrases such as "to have
   a grudge against," "He laughs best who laughs last."

4. Translate a paragraph to French.

This was a test designed for prospective foreign language
teachers. As can be seen, pronunciation was still tested by
pen and paper, there was no auditory or spoken element, no
question that called for free expression. In 1932 almost 30
percent of the candidates failed to attain the passing mark of
65 percent on this test, and many others were barely above
the passing level. The very conservative format was not irrelevant to the fact that Price, New York's supervisor for education, had been at the forefront in opposing the conclusions of
the Coleman report. It is a reminder that changes in testing
work very slowly through a calcified system. Price, being
based in the secondary schools, had a very low opinion of
university faculty, be it as teachers or testers. In his words, "It
is incontestable that most college professors have a horror of
teaching the language" (1933, 85).

The United States foreign language testing tradition has for
a long time differed from that of Europe in the low esteem
placed on the use of translation as a testing device. The translation format was never even considered by those who elaborated the tests for the Modern Foreign Language Study. There

are very few references in the testing literature to translation. One exception is provided by Haden and Stalnaker (1934), who carried out a study aimed at improving the reliability of scoring for translation tests. Their solution was to break the translation into sections for scoring. Though this was hardly novel, the same could not be said of their suggestion that a properly sectioned passage for translation into English could be reliably scored even by people who did not know the foreign language. This assertion appears to have gone untested and remains unsubstantiated.

Testing Culture

Foreign language educators have traditionally offered many abstract goals ancillary to the teaching of a particular language. They have spoken in terms of wider cultural benefits such as appreciation of another country's worldview and values, as well as of its art and history. Indeed Coleman's second goal, subordinate only to reading, was the imparting of "especial interest in the foreign language and its people, considerable knowledge of its past and present, and a broadening attitude toward other civilizations than our own." The College Board's list of goals adopted in 1932 states that "an important ultimate aim for all pupils is to enable them to understand foreign civilizations. To this end it is recommended that attention be paid increasingly . . . to the geography, history, institutions, and customs of the countries in question" (1941). Nevertheless, in any survey of the history of foreign language education it is evident that these abstract goals have rarely been the object of testing. This must diminish belief in the sincerity of those who affirm faith in such outcomes. In the 1920s Robert Fife noted ironically, "It is not possible to escape the inference that the teacher is more optimistic about the success of his pupils in those fields which he cannot test, the fields of transfer values and of the formation of desirable intellectual and social habits, than in those fields in which he tests at regular intervals."

An exception to this came in February 1937, when a formal discussion on this topic was held in New Orleans by a panel of language course supervisors. Reviewing the state of foreign language teaching then current, the supervisors expressed dissatisfaction with the narrow scope of testing, especially with the fact that testing ignored the broad humanistic goals that supervisors ascribed to foreign language education. The 1930s did see some efforts to tackle the question of how such nonlinguistic outcomes of foreign language study were to be measured. Though the College Boards commission had called for increased attention to the teaching of the geography, history, and general culture of foreign countries, the boards' examinations were slow to incorporate these areas. However, James Tharp (1934) of Ohio State University devised a *Test in French Civilization* that grouped questions under headings such as geography and travel, history, fine arts and music, science, and literature. The format used was basically that of matching. Miller (1935) reported on a somewhat similar *Test of French Life and Culture* developed at Kansas State Teachers College, a center of interest in culture teaching. This contained one hundred questions on French geography, history, government, and art. Forty of these required student input, e.g.:

On what island was Napoleon born?

The format of the remaining sixty questions was multiple choice or matching. An analysis of the results showed that the easiest question (answered correctly by 97 percent of 218 junior college and high school students) was:

Name one Frenchman who aided the thirteen colonies during the American revolution.

The most difficult question (correctly matched by only 11 percent) was:

Name an important [French] poet of the first part of the nineteenth century.

Russo (1940) offered a similar multiple-choice test of Italian civilization, and Peebles (1937) offered one for German. Buda (1931) wrote a master's thesis on devising a cultural test. Others articulated doubts about using new-type testing formats to test culture, believing that culture was "of all tests the least suited to the present fashion for examinations which can be marked by clerks who have no knowledge of the subject" (Edward quoted in Buros 1940).

It is somewhat startling that the language requirement that many universities impose on candidates for the doctorate has received so little attention from language testers. The issue did attract a certain amount of interest in the 1930s. Fuchs (1932) wrote a Ph.D. dissertation on the doctoral language requirement, surveying sixty-four universities as to what Ph.D. candidates in other disciplines were expected to know of a foreign language. Thirty-nine university departments took part in a separate survey of practices used to test the foreign language doctoral reading requirement (Frantz 1939). Findings in all cases indicated an extraordinary disparity of practices. Some universities designed their own reading tests, others used a standardized form such as part of the Cooperative tests. In some universities the student had to translate, in others to answer questions on a written passage. The University of Chicago was one of the few institutions to take the Ph.D. language requirement sufficiently seriously to devise a comprehensive test (Stalnaker and Eggan 1934). The percentage of students reported as passing the tests ranged from 85 percent down to 1 percent. Definitions of "a reading knowledge" varied widely from department to department. The question has lain untouched for the last six decades, peripheral to all save those Ph.D. students who have to take such qualifying language examinations. Graduate Record Examinations in foreign languages began in 1939. Their use of a multiple-choice format posed the question of whether such a format could take account of the complex and sophisticated skills needed for graduate study.

Another area of relevance to assessment that has neverthe-less been all but ignored for many years by testers is that of the form of the comprehensive examinations that a number of universities require their students to take for graduation. Jones (1937) evaluated a wide sample of such examinations in for-eign languages. He discovered that many different techniques were in use, the large majority being essay-type or discursive questions, with little over 1 percent being of the "objective" type. Generally the German examinations showed more in-terest in form and specific information, while Romance lan-guage questions allowed for more discussion and gave sufficient latitude to investigate broader philosophical interre-lationships.

As was the case in the 1920s, the only aspect of oral testing that received any attention in the years before the Second World War was that of pronunciation. The exception to this was Harvard, which during the 1930s required Spanish stu-dents to take a fifteen-minute oral examination at the end of each semester (Hall 1936). Otherwise no tests sought to test grammar, vocabulary, or overall communicative ability orally. Even pronunciation testing was uncommon. Haley (1940) described a test in use at the College of St. Catherine in Min-nesota. The elicitation mechanism consisted of the student's reading a French passage aloud. Judges marked right or wrong for particular words, also grading for elision and into-nation. A considerable amount of pronunciation testing con-tinued to require no oral output. Kaulfers (1937) described a rather complicated test that required a high level of metalin-guistic intuition:

> In each line below is a series of five words. All words except
> one contain the same vowel sound. In the parentheses you
> are to indicate the symbol for this sound. Then in the blank
> space to the left you are to write the word that does not con-
> tain this sound.
>
> décédé   effort   parlerai   derrière   chez

The answer sought was *derrière*, presumably for the sound represented by the second *è*.

Each year James Tharp of Ohio State University published his bibliography of work on language teaching and methodology in the *Modern Language Journal*. As part of this bibliography he analyzed the published literature by category, using about a dozen different headings. This enabled him to set out a hierarchy as to what topics had attracted most research attention for a particular year. Testing was always quite high on that list, reaching fourth place in 1934, seventh in 1935, and fifth in 1936. Combining the three years into a cumulative bibliography of 454 items of research, 40 dealt with testing, a large number of these dwelling on matters of placement and sectioning (McDonald and Tharp 1938).

Testing matters were beginning to attract the attention of students seeking topics for doctoral dissertations. Apart from Walker's study mentioned earlier, Clarence Ficken in 1937 presented his Ph.D. dissertation also at the University of Wisconsin, titled "Intercorrelations of Part Scores in Foreign Language Tests," in which he ran a statistical analysis of scores on the Cooperative French Test. Walter Kaulfers, who was to have a long and distinguished career in foreign language education, in 1933 defended his dissertation on prognosis testing for junior high school Spanish at Stanford. He argued that no available prognosis test was particularly useful for this purpose. Indeed, prognosis testing attracted the interest of a number of graduate students. Berttine's 1928 master's thesis at the University of Southern California was titled "Means of Predicting Success in First Year College Foreign Language Work," while in 1933 Raymond Brock turned in his thesis at the same institution, titled "An Experimental Evaluation of Various Bases for Prognosis in Spanish." He found that the ability to spell in English was a good predictor of foreign language success. Laura Canty, in her 1935 master's thesis, "Twenty-Five Case Studies of Outstanding Successes and Failures in French Classes at New Jersey State Teachers College," reported that her investigation had shown what she termed possession of "imagination" to be the best predictor. Those who did poorly in French all lacked "imagination." Lau (1933) offered an empirical study that seemed to at least partially validate the Symonds Prognosis Test. The Symonds test was also partially validated by Richardson (1933). Greenberg (1938) wrote his Ph.D. dissertation on the correlation between IQ and success in foreign language. He found a rather low correlation, somewhat against the prevailing feeling that intelligence was vital. Evans (1937) wrote her master's thesis at Ohio State on the question of the reliability of raters of pronunciation tests, probably the first academic study of foreign language test reliability to be carried out. These years saw the development of distance education, based on classes given over the radio. Students who took Ohio State University's language courses by radio mailed their tests to the university to be graded, enclosing stamped, addressed envelopes (Meiden 1942).

Though the foregoing might indicate otherwise, the 1930s were overall a time of some torpor in foreign language teaching and testing. In fact, the decline was manifested in physical terms; the great figures of foreign language controversy of the 1920s were already beginning to fall. Price, the influential New York supervisor, died in 1936; his adversary, Algernon Coleman, died three years later. After Price's death the reading approach gained considerable ground in New York State. Despite the interest in the question of placement, there appears to have been little connection between high schools and universities. North Carolina, where the University of North Carolina's syllabus "A Two-Year Course in Spanish" was disseminated throughout the state's high schools, was an exception in this regard (Stoudemire 1937).

Nationally the decline in student numbers continued and would persist for decades after. Even at the height of popularity of modern languages in the 1920s, Latin still exceeded all foreign languages combined in high school enrollment. The attrition persisted because a vast number of those students who undertook a foreign language course dropped it after a year or a semester, long before any usable proficiency was gained. The teaching of foreign language came under attack from those who saw it as ineffective and irrelevant. Proponents of "general language" called instead for the teaching of courses about language and languages, rather than of a specific language. As Spaulding (1933, 135) put it, "The teaching of modern languages tends, under present conditions, to be one of the most wasteful enterprises of the American secondary school." In language testing, as in so much else in the society of the 1930s, little of the ebullience of the 1920s remained.

4

The Second World War

World War I had been a vital catalyst for the testing boom experienced by the United States in the 1920s. The impact of World War II on foreign language teaching proved to be no less dramatic. Even before the United States entered the Second World War, the realization that conflict was likely, if not imminent, provided a spur for the training of personnel. In 1941 the Rockefeller Foundation, through the American Council of Learned Societies (ACLS), created a program designed to provide a pool of persons skilled in the use of foreign languages. This project was oriented toward the less commonly taught languages, and in its summer offering of 1942 fifty-six courses were provided in twenty-six languages. Eighteen colleges or universities took part, providing instruction for some seven hundred students. In its methodology the Intensive Language Program drew to a large extent on the theories and practices of American structuralism, at the time the dominant intellectual base of American linguistics. The theoretical tradition on which the teaching methodology was based went as far back as Boas's *Handbook of American Indian Languages* (1911) and Bloomfield's *Introduction to the Study of Language* (1914), as well as Bloomfield's later work.

The ACLS language teaching program of 1942 remains noteworthy for the fact that in it for the first time in the United States language teaching and theoretical linguistics drew rather close together. Linguists who had hitherto worked in more theoretical or research areas were called upon to turn their attention to devising language teaching methods. Naturally enough they tended to use models of language learning that had proved useful in field work—recourse to native informants and repetition, for example. The Intensive Language Program was thus innovative not only when measured by the number of new courses introduced, but also when judged in terms of its avowedly "scientific" approach to the study of language and language learning. Those who designed the Intensive Language Program claimed that its achievements were "epoch-making, not only when measured by the considerable number of new courses introduced, but perhaps even more when judged in terms of increased experiment with and advertising of intensive methods, improvement of implementation, and scientific study of linguistic phenomena" (Angiolillo 1947, 162).

Once the United States had entered the war, the need for skilled personnel in a wide range of activities was apparent. To this end the Provost Marshal General's office created the Army Specialized Training Program (ASTP), to offer instruction in several areas, particularly engineering and premedical. About 140,000 military personnel received instruction under the ASTP. Of these, some 12,000 were assigned to the Division of Foreign Area and Language Studies. The ASTP administered over five hundred language courses in a wide variety of languages, both those already commonly taught and those that were not. Its aims and curriculum were markedly opposed to those that had dominated language teaching in the academic environment during the previous decades. The emphasis was on oral communication, a goal that had lost so much ground during the previous decade's enthronement of the reading method.

The army never set out a specific methodology for the courses, and thus the participating institutions were free to develop their own teaching practices. In the "Curriculum No. 71" of the Division of Foreign Area and Language Studies, the objective of the ASTP was defined as "to impart to the trainee a command of the colloquial spoken form of a language and to give the trainee a sound knowledge of the area in which the language is used" (Angiolillo 1947, 32). Courses sought to give the functional ability to communicate in a foreign language environment and to understand those aspects of its culture that might be relevant to the prosecution of the war. Classes were held in civilian institutions, such as universities and colleges. In fact, participants in the ASTP theoretically were full students of the particular institution they were attending.

The army was keen on continual assessment and re-sectioning, and indeed men were promoted or demoted on the basis of their test scores. Thus there was a lot of testing conducted as part of the ASTP. One writer actually criticized what he termed the "unreasonable amount" of testing, which he charged was "enervating both to students and faculty" (Herbert 1944). Another GI reported that ASTP students felt that testing was over-emphasized, but that insufficient oral tests were administered (Reiden 1945). By and large the army appears to have ignored the need to develop testing and grading practices to reflect the new communicative goals.

Though grammar was to be taught merely as a means to an end, it is striking that most of the ASTP testing persisted in gauging grammatical knowledge rather than seeking to assess how students' communicative skills were developing. Thus the MLA committee, which carried out an extensive review of the program in 1944, reported that "the best tests have been found to be the standard devices" (1944). These "standard devices" included tests such as the Columbia and Cooperative tests. In some institutions, however, tests that were not multiple choice were employed, such as paraphrasing spoken anecdotes or situations, oral responses to questions, dictation, and written responses to auditory comprehension questions. The committee did recommend the creation of "new devices for objectively testing aural and oral proficiency," but because the ASTP program was short-lived, a full-scale testing revolution never had time to occur within the ASTP.

Though the army did not prescribe one single philosophy of testing, it did tend to encourage criterion-referenced rather than norm-referenced tests. The army suggested the establishment of two criterion-based levels of proficiency for the purposes of rating an individual's language ability:

> 1. Trainees who have satisfied the institutional authorities that they can both comprehend and speak the language as well as a person with the same amount of formal schooling should speak his mother tongue will be . . . designated on availability reports as "expert."

> 2. Trainees who have satisfied the institutional authorities that they can readily comprehend the language as spoken by one adult native to another and can speak the language well enough to be intelligible to natives on non-technical subjects of military importance will be . . . designated on availability reports as "competent." (Ghigo 1943)

This scale has an important place in the history of testing, especially in the nonacademic environment, because it marks the first use of a functional rather than grammatical criterion of proficiency in foreign language. However, the scale never gained wide acceptance among those conducting the ASTP. Other rating methods were preferred, such as designations of "excellent/good/fair," or even more conservative scales such as the conventional one hundred-point range. The fact that ASTP students were thought of as regular students of their particular institution and were in many cases receiving college credit from that institution fostered a tendency for instructors to persist with the testing techniques and grading standards they had used prior to the war.

There were some instances of more innovative testing practices. Harris (1944) describes auditory tests used in the ASTP at the University of Wisconsin. In addition to a dictation, in one section the instructor read out a sentence, and students simply translated:

> Voulez-vous faire une promenade?

Other sections of the examination called on students to write answers to spoken passages, the answers being either in English or the target language. One such question was

Avez-vous acheté un journal aujourd'hui?

Much of the experimental testing activity was centered at Queens College in New York. Here, for instance, an oral examination was administered and recorded on phonograph. In addition to standard techniques such as conversation and translator situations, the test employed many of the materials employed in the teaching itself, such as cartoons and visual aids (Angiolillo 1947, 159).

Many persons associated with the army's language program were undoubtedly aware of the need for new testing formats. In 1944, Walter Kaulfers, in reviewing the kinds of language tests demanded by the special environment of the Second World War, listed the following as the tester's goal:

> The nature of the individual test items should be such as to provide specific, recognizable evidence of the examinee's readiness to perform in a life-situation, where lack of ability to understand and speak extemporaneously might be a serious handicap to safety and comfort, or to the effective execution of military responsibilities. (1944, 137)

To this end, Kaulfers supported the use of such items as "How would you tell a Spanish-speaking native to get a doctor? How would you ask him to change a ten-dollar bill?" These were literally survival tests, and so they focused on a restricted range of grammatical structures, especially imperatives and interrogatives. Notwithstanding this, Kaulfers's view of the function of a language test, as to measure "readiness to perform in a life-situation," provided a good short definition of what a language proficiency test seeks to measure.

The Army Specialized Training Program had a very brief existence, lasting scarcely one academic year. On 18 February 1944 the War Department announced the cancellation of most of the ASTP courses. It cited reasons of "imperative military necessity"—in reality the need to avail itself of a source to replenish the personnel losses incurred in Europe and Asia. A full evaluation of the content and achievements of the ASTP language program remains to be drawn up elsewhere.

The initial euphoria of the popular press that "linguistic science" had finally devised a foolproof method for learning foreign languages was obviously overblown. In contrast, the tone of the MLA committee's report was more measured: "A considerable percent of the trainees did acquire the ability to express themselves with fluency and reasonable accuracy in the foreign language . . . and a high level of ability to understand the spoken language as employed by different native speakers under circumstances representing normal speaking conditions" (Doyle 1944). Of course, the ASTP had many advantages over the current high schools or colleges. There was a fair amount of selectivity as to student intake, and those who took part did so in an atmosphere of military discipline. Indeed, it has often been observed that the army method's fondness for drill-drill was not unconnected with the army setting itself. Large blocks of time were allotted to work in and out of class, and class size was generally small. Because attendance at an ASTP program was considered a privilege, motivation to do well and stay the course was high. The alternative—a possible combat posting—was not universally considered attractive.

As the goals of the program were explicitly stated in terms of the military's ability to function in the foreign language environment, a proper evaluation of the success of the program would be based on evidence of how well ASTP graduates were able to discharge their duties through the medium of the foreign language they had studied. However, many ASTP graduates, because of the shifting manpower needs of the war, never had the opportunity to exercise their foreign language abilities in the field. As one commentator pointed out, the apparent success of the program "did not prevent the Army from sending to France infantrymen who had been beautifully trained to speak Japanese" (*Science* 1944). The others, those who did have an opportunity to use their foreign language training, were so far-flung and used their languages in such disparate situations that no general evaluation of their competence was ever carried out. It appears that no studies were carried out of how well those who learned foreign languages in the ASTP performed on the standardized tests then available.

Not all the testing yielded by the army's involvement in foreign language teaching was representative of the best of the day. Toward the end of the war the testing branch of the Armed Forces Institute issued a series of standardized tests of such things as French grammar, reading comprehension, and vocabulary. These tests were not a success and were severely criticized by the reviewers in the *Third Mental Measurements Yearbook*. Apart from poor production quality—there were many misprints—items were tested out of context, incorrect French was used, and many items tested not just the foreign language but things such as intelligence or logic. Nevertheless, the military's involvement with language teaching and testing during the Second World War represented the beginning of a vital movement in the history of foreign language testing in the United States. From the emergency needs occasioned by the Second World War stemmed the strand of the American language testing tradition that stresses the holistic and functional use of language in authentic settings. This view of testing, for several decades confined to military and governmental agencies, is today in one form or another dominant in language testing generally.

While academic work in testing was obviously restricted during the war, the 1940s are important as marking the introduction of techniques of factor analysis to theoretical testing research. In 1941 John Carroll completed his dissertation at the University of Minnesota. He published his research in an article in which he offered a factor analysis of native-speaker abilities in English. This interest was to come to fruition for Carroll in his work on aptitude testing two decades later. Factor analysis also formed the theme of Wittenborn and Larsen's 1944 analysis of scores on examinations in German. In stating their belief that a large element of the variance was attributable to "a language factor," they presaged the great debates of decades later as to the unitary or divisible nature of language competence. The war years were important, too, in that 1942 saw the final death of the old-style College Board examinations, and their replacement by the board's achievement tests. Henceforth the College Board would not seek to influence curriculum through its tests, but rather reflect curricular diversity through examinations that were not specific to any syllabus.

The only major application of the ASTP's work to the war and postwar academic environment came in the form of Agard and Dunkel's investigation (1948) of the situation of foreign language teaching. This important survey of the state of language teaching, commonly known as the Chicago study, began as early as 1944. It provided a compelling picture of the position of teaching and testing during these years. The authors concluded that there was no consensus among teachers regarding what to test or how to test it: "As for actual tests of oral production, we know of none in published form for general use" (1948, 55). Faced with this gap, Agard and Dunkel were obliged to create their own tests. These tests built upon the more innovative elements of the ASTP testing and proved an important affirmation of the break from the old testing tradition. Some of the novel test formats developed at Queens College in New York, but never brought to fruition during the war, provided the groundwork for the tests used in the Investigation of Second Language Teaching. Communicative ability—intelligibility, as the researchers called it—rather than grammar was the goal. One part of the test used a series of pictures, to be described by the candidate. The second part, called "sustained speech," required the student to discourse without interruption on a topic assigned to him on the spot, such as:

> Lower level: You are talking with a Spanish-speaking person who has never been to the United States. Describe to him the town or city in which you live. [If further stimulus is necessary before time is up]: This person is also interested in what a North American home looks like. Describe to him the home in which you live.

Upper level: You have met a young German in Europe who seems to you to have the makings of an outstanding American citizen. You resolve to try to convince him that he should emigrate to the United States. Talk to him about the United States so that you may help him decide whether he would like to come. [If further stimulus is necessary before time is up]: Your young German friend is interested in American schools. Describe to him life at the school you attend.

Part 3 consisted of a directed conversation, with stimuli on phonograph disc. The student heard two voices on the record; one was in the target language, while the other directed the candidate how to respond. So the recorded native speaker might say : "¿Cómo está usted?", whereupon the English voice on the record would say: "Tell him you're fine and ask him how he is."

All three parts were scored on a rating scale, going from 0 to 2. Scoring for parts 1 and 3 of the test was holistic, with a rating scale based on success in getting the message across. Part 2 was scored on a more grammatically based scale, with four separate factors to be scored: fluency, vocabulary, pronunciation/enunciation, and grammatical correctness. Agard and Dunkel built on the best of the wartime innovations, and their formats looked forward to modern tests. The kinds of testing goals they articulated have ever since typified the practice of United States governmental bodies. The provision of scales presaged the use of scales in the Foreign Service Institute, as was also the case with the separate scoring for different factors and with the directed-interpreting part of the test. The crediting of success in "getting the message across" marked quite a change from the right/wrong grammatically oriented tests of previous years, while the resort to "situations" (including some involving folk customs and etiquette in the target culture) is still seen in the ACTFL/ETS situation cards.

Generally Agard and Dunkel were less than satisfied with the state of foreign language teaching as they found it. The famous Harvard report of 1945, "General Education in a Free Society," had recommended that foreign language study need not form part of any basic college curriculum. The decline in high school foreign language enrollments had continued during the war. Neither students taught by traditional methods, nor those who learned languages in experimental army-type settings, showed a satisfactory degree of proficiency. As one step toward remedying this, Agard and Dunkel made the very farsighted suggestion that national proficiency descriptions be written, to be used as goals in language teaching and testing. No action was taken on this recommendation. Indeed, a reading of the testing literature of the early 1950s shows that Agard and Dunkel's work failed to be assimilated within the profession. Though the war probably showed up the inadequacies of the reading method, no fundamental change in testing practices in high school or college grew out of the innovations brought about in the 1940s. It was to be many years before the academic world would catch up with the best elements of ASTP foreign language teaching and testing.

5

Audiolingualism

In 1952 Edna Furness reviewed the literature on foreign language testing for her doctoral dissertation entitled "An Experiment in Objective Measurement of Aural Comprehension of Spanish." She concluded pessimistically that there were still few auditory tests available, and no speaking test. Furness concurred with what Agard and Dunkel had found in the late 1940s: there was a dearth of tests that might measure overall communicative ability in a foreign language. In accounting for the failure to teach or test the ability to speak a foreign language, Agard and Dunkel adduced essentially the same reasons as had been put forward decades before. They pointed out that the large class size of the time, often as many as forty students in a section, was a major obstacle to a concentration on oral ability. This was aggravated by the short length of language courses and by the low level of oral ability among the teaching population itself, many of whom were products of the reading emphasis of the 1930s and 1940s. In addition, because international transport and communication remained, if not difficult, at least expensive, there seemed no need to teach or test an accomplishment that might never be used. Far wiser, it appeared, was to view language learning as mental training and as a means of introduction to the great literatures of the world (Agard and Dunkel 1948).

Around this time a representative of the College Boards was gloomy about the prospects for oral or auditory tests. He believed that the introduction of an auditory element would necessitate the purchase of up to twelve thousand "talking machines." He termed oral examinations a "frightening prospect," though he was able to visualize a time when an oral exam might be carried out by having the student record his answers on a disc. He ended on an even more lugubrious note, with the suggestion that testing administration problems might go away if the current decline in high school foreign language enrollment continued (Walsh 1953). In this light it seemed that the road taken by the army language programs during the Second World War had led nowhere. The goals of language teaching in high school and college remained unaltered from the prewar days, and hence the tests in use had not needed to be changed.

However, there was evidence already visible of the beginnings of a new and invigorated teaching and testing movement. Nineteen forty-eight saw the founding of the Educational Testing Service, an institution that was to play a truly central role in foreign language testing. In 1952 the Modern Language Association developed a renewed interest in language pedagogy, forming the MLA Foreign Language Program. These years also brought the production of large numbers of tests by the U.S. military. The Army Language Proficiency Tests, which subsequently developed into the respected Defense Language Proficiency Tests, were unsuccessful as tests (Petersen and Cartier 1975), but at least they maintained alive the tradition of military involvement.

In 1951, building on the work of Agard and Dunkel's Chicago investigation, a group of foreign language teachers formed the Yale-Barnard Conference on the Teaching of French. This in 1954 became the Northeast Conference on the Teaching of Foreign Languages. Nelson Brooks and others created the Yale-Barnard Aural Test in French, a test that was innovative because the entire examination was in French, even the directions. This test was later taken over by the College Board to become in 1954 the board's first auditory test, probably the first test ever to be termed "listening comprehension." It attempted to test a wide range of registers of the target language, from informal conversation to lectures or short excerpts from plays. Formats ranged from answering whether the heard stimulus was true or false to deciding whether the second of two remarks heard was a logical response to the first. Such formats cut out the influence of extraneous variables.

> Könnten Sie mir, bitte, einen Hundermarkschein wechseln?
> Leider nicht, aber nebenan en ist eine Bank.

Other formats required students to select a picture that described what they heard in the stimulus. A rather new-type item employed brief dialogues and called for students to identify general elements such as where or between whom such a conversation was taking place:

> Hélène, écrivez au tableau les phrases de la leçon d'aujourd'hui.

> Je regrette, Monsieur, hier soir je ne me sentais pas bien, et je n'ai pas fait le devoir.

Cette conversation se passe entre:

   a) un homme d'affaires et sa secrétaire

   b) un médecin et une malade

   c) un professeur et son élève

   d) un garçon de café et une cliente

Such items were not word-based, as many previous listening comprehension tests had been. They sought to duplicate situations that might occur in real life. A further example of the search to mimic natural language processes came in the College Board's decision to allow stimuli to be heard only once. The Yale-Barnard prototype had permitted stimuli and questions to be repeated once, but the College Boards decided that this encouraged bad listening habits and opted instead to include a greater number of items in order to use the extra time gained by abolishing repetitions. Furthering the search for authenticity, often well-known foreign actors or broadcasting personalities agreed to record the listening sections to "contribute to a better understanding of their native language and culture in America."

Stabb (1955) reported on work in oral testing at Colgate University. The Colgate Oral Language Examination used photographs and drawings to elicit the foreign language. Students also had to retell orally in their own words a story they had read in the foreign language. Grading was carried out on the basis of a series of descriptive statements defining supposed levels of ability. Interesting work in testing was also being carried out at the United States Air Force Academy in San Antonio, where the institution was faced with training foreign airmen. Buechel (1957) described the "quality control" approach to language testing employed by the U.S. Air Force. Verbal descriptions of ability, called rating standards, were employed to categorize learners' proficiency in English as a second language. These were assigned numerical values, with scales typically ranging from 1 to 5 or 0 to 6. These numerical values were similar to those employed at the Foreign Service Institute, though the operational descriptions differed.

The 1950s were the first decade in which the U.S. government became involved in funding language testing research. In 1954 Congress created the Cooperative Research Program of the United States Department of Education, and later the National Defense Education Act of 1958. In 1955 a national assembly of foreign language educators and the Modern Language Association recommended standards of linguistic proficiency for teachers, defined as "minimal," "good," and "superior." Scales were listed in seven areas: listening, speaking, reading, and writing, plus language analysis, culture, and professional preparation. The standards for speaking were:

> Minimal: Ability to read aloud and to talk on prepared topics (e.g. for classroom situations) without obvious faltering and to use the common expressions needed for getting around in the foreign country, speaking with a pronunciation understandable to a native.

Good: Ability to talk with a native without making glaring mistakes, and with a command of vocabulary and syntax sufficient to express one's thoughts in conversation at normal speed with reasonably good pronunciation.

Superior: Ability to speak fluently, approximating native speech in vocabulary, intonation and pronunciation. Ability to exchange ideas and to be at ease in social situations. (Starr 1962, 38)

These standards were later incorporated into the Modern Language Association's effort to create national proficiency tests. In conjunction with the Educational Testing Service, the MLA mounted a major project in the late 1950s to develop a series of tests in foreign languages (including Russian) and teacher preparation. The MLA in 1960 administered some twenty-six thousand language tests on a pilot basis. This figure rose the following year to forty-three thousand. These numbers constituted the most expansive mass testing to be mounted since the 1920s, and the scale of this work has never been matched since the 1960s. These projects came to fruition in the form of the MLA Proficiency Tests for Advanced Students published 1962, and the MLA Cooperative Tests in 1964 (Clark 1965). The MLA Proficiency Test had items such as the following, for French listening comprehension:

Pourquoi ne m'avez-vous pas dit que la représentation ne commencerait pas à l'heure habituelle?

a) Je n'en savais rien

b) Non, elle n'a pas commencé à l'heure

c) Oui, c'est moi qui vous l'ai dit

d) Après le lever du rideau

This did not show much adherence to the notion of testing one thing at a time, but the exam's speaking section was more faithful in this regard. In this, the student merely repeated sentences heard on tape. Each sentence spoken by the master voice contained two critical sounds. The scorers agreed to give a right score only if the candidate's production of the critical sound was an exact imitation of the master voice. Any mistake in the utterance other than the critical sounds was to be ignored (Paquette and Tollinger 1968, 30).

In 1955 the College Board agreed to sponsor the Advanced Placement Program (AP), which had been created a few years earlier as a cooperative effort among twelve colleges and twenty-six secondary schools. The College Board contracted with ETS to administer and score the examinations. Initially the AP examinations for foreign languages were restricted to literature, though the examination included listening comprehension tests (on an optional basis) for the first time in 1960. These were written questions on taped passages. It was to be much later before AP exams were offered specifically in foreign language as well as literature.

In 1964 ETS and the College Board instituted the College Level Examination Program (CLEP) with the goal of allowing students to gain credit for college-level achievement acquired outside the conventional college classroom, though it was to be more than a decade later before foreign language tests were offered by CLEP. CLEP posed questions that were never properly addressed by the foreign language teaching profession, namely the admissibility of granting double credit for the same work—once in high school, then in college—through CLEP. And, in a deeper sense, it questioned the place of foreign language in the tradition of the humanistic and liberal education. As M. P. Hagiwara wrote when reviewing the CLEP (1972), "And what of the intellectual content of the college language curriculum? One certainly does not teach language skills in a vacuum, for the attainment of language proficiency is only part of the goals of the curriculum."

The 1950s saw the creation of applied linguistics as a discipline. A concrete manifestation of this was the setting up of the Center for Applied Linguistics in 1959. For the first time in the history of foreign language testing, the 1950s and 1960s saw the provision of a theory of language and language testing to underpin what was being attempted in practice. The

theory was founded on ideas associated with American structuralist linguistics. Though often divergent (Hymes and
Fought 1975), these ideas tended to be characterized by the
belief that languages should be seen as independent structures
that were best studied through analysis of their component
parts. Structuralists tended to share a faith in a methodology of
analysis and classification and sought to isolate and list the
discrete elements of the languages they studied. To such an
extent was this the case that Chomsky and Halle (1968, 402
n) rather disparagingly labeled this concentration "taxonomic
linguistics."

Structural linguistics applied to the classroom produced
audiolingualism, its teaching practices and learning theories
rooted to a large extent in behaviorist models of learning.
Learning was thought to follow the stimulus-response pattern,
with repetition and practice leading to the inculcation of new
habits of language behavior. With Charles Fries (1945) one
already sees how this will be applied to the classroom, but it
was Robert Lado who applied structuralism in a systematic
way to foreign language testing. In Lado's words (1964,4):

> The lowly power of habit is the support of the distinctively
> human gift of language. We can in this sense speak of lan-
> guage as a conventionalized, highly complex system of habits
> which functions as a human instrument of communication.

For Lado, the difficulty in learning a foreign language resulted from the very newness of these habits—the fact that they
differ from the "old" habits learned as first language. A second
language is difficult because it is different. Lado in fact dubbed
as "nonproblems" for the learner those structural areas that do
not differ between the first and second language. These
elements "are transferred from the native language, and
because they function satisfactorily, they do not have to be
learned anew." The "problems" were thus the true domain of
the language test. In Lado's aphorism, "Testing the problems
is testing the language" (1964, 20).

If learning a foreign language entailed mastering a finite list of "problems" until the entire set of sounds and structures had been acquired, it followed that the learner's proficiency could best be gauged by estimating the quantity of these sounds and structures that he had at any given time learned as habit. If one could break language up in order to teach it, it was logical that one might also break it up in order to test it. As Nelson Brooks put it (1950):

> If we are not able to inspect the wall in its finished form, can we not examine the bricks our workman is using, see whether he has mixed his mortar properly, whether he handles his trowel deftly, whether he remembers to lay one brick on two and is able to follow a plumb line? And, if all these things are satisfactory, then can we not assume that his wall, when finished, will meet the specifications of the building code?

Lado (1953, 32) actually opposed the provision of context in the creation of foreign language testing items and argued in favor of short rather than long stimuli. In this his testing formats marked a return to those instituted by the multiple-choice testers of the 1920s. Lado maintained that "continuous discourse may actually give away the answers instead of making them more difficult." The creation of lists of likely "problem" areas arising from the learner's need to acquire new habits provided fertile ground for applied linguists in the 1960s (Politzer and Staubach 1961; Stockwell and Bowen 1965). Theoreticians such as these maintained, following Lado, that an analysis that contrasted the native and foreign languages was indispensable when drawing up areas and elements to be covered in testing. Rather than devise, say, a test of French, the tester's true task could better be defined as to devise a test of French for native speakers of English; indeed, putting it more precisely, to devise a test of some element of French for English speakers. To this end they sought to set up a hierarchy of difficulty that would express the quantity of negative transfer suffered between L1 and L2. This would be set against a hierarchy of importance of elements in the target language— what was termed the functional load of particular items.

John Carroll (1961) coined the term by which this procedure has since been known—the "discrete-point" approach. The conceptual framework of the classical discrete-point test can be thought of as being composed of two axes. One axis embodied the skill to be tested—broadly speaking, the four principal skills of listening, speaking, reading, and writing. The other represented the four major classificatory components used by the structuralists: phonology (orthography in the case of the written word), morphology, syntax, and lexicon. Within this axis, there was room for ever greater subdivision into the discrete points of the language. The domain of the test can be considered as the intersection of lines drawn on each axis, where a specific kind of knowledge shows itself in a specific kind of behavior. A wide range of testing methods could be used, e.g., multiple choice, completion, matching, true/false, etc. Theoretically, any particular skill could be measured by just about any of these methods, though it appears that many of the possible permutations were never tried out in the real world. Thus, one could not properly describe a test of this kind as a test of Spanish, to take an example. One could only speak of measuring a particular language element as evinced in a particular skill—trilled /r/ in speech, for example, or the imperfect/preterite distinction in reading. One could only "test one thing at a time." Taxonomic linguistics had given birth to taxonomic testing.

As a teaching method audiolingualism never delivered the results that some of its theoreticians had promised. The psycholinguistic underpinnings of audiolingualism received a lethal blow from Chomsky's new paradigm (1959), which demonstrated that behaviorism provided an inadequate theory of language learning. On the practical level, studies such as the Pennsylvania Project (Smith 1970) showed that audiolingualism achieved results no better than a more traditional methodology. There was no empirical backing for the claims of the audiolingualists as to the effectiveness of their teaching methods. Research also showed that audiolingual testing tenets were weak in their foundations. In the first place, contrastive analysis in its "strong version" purported to predict learner behavior. There was, however, no body of research evidence to support this claim. Indeed, it is somewhat surprising that no significant empirical validation studies of contrastive analysis were carried out in the 1960s, given its adherents' pride in the "scientific" status of their methodology. It is fruitless to search the contrastive literature of the time for anything more convincing than anecdote or impression. Hierarchies such as those of Stockwell and Bowen were based on impression, not on data. In fact, as early as 1966, at the Northeast Conference, up to that point a stronghold of audiolingualism, widespread dissatisfaction with the empirical basis of contrastive analysis was expressed (Ferguson 1966). Another flaw in the contrastive analysis/structuralist position rested in the kind of corpora dealt with. While structuralists were loud in proclaiming the primacy of speech over writing, most of the evidence they analyzed was written, not spoken.

Disenchantment grew as the decade progressed. In 1968 John Carroll wrote of finding a test composed of "a more or less random assortment" of "intuitively good" items to be more valid than one explicitly drawn up on the basis of contrastive analysis (56). In the early 1970s the anticontrastive analysis dam burst. A number of researchers, of whom the foremost was John Oller, showed that the "strong" or predictive version of contrastive analysis was untenable. This left the weak version, namely, that contrastive analysis could shed some light on some learner behavior, irrefutable but impotent.

Aside from its nonexistent empirical basis, the contrastive analysis theory suffered from two interrelated logical flaws. First, if languages are so different, as the structuralists had stressed, how could they be legitimately compared or contrasted? In fact, the more two languages were different, the harder it should be to make meaningful comparisons or contrasts, and so the theory coped worst with those cases with which it should have coped best. Each language should be studied on its own terms, said the structuralists, but on which language's terms should a contrastive analysis be made?

The second theoretical anomaly in contrastive analysis was pointed out as early as 1962 by John Upshur. He noticed that once the individual begins to learn, he is no longer the "pure native speaker" demanded by the theory: "All of what he has learned will have facilitation or interference effects upon what has not yet been taught" (116). This was an early depiction of what was later to be termed "interlanguage" (Selinker 1974), a transitional competence in the target language composed of sets of hypotheses about that language, based upon observations of both the target language and the native language. Contrastive analysis, if it were to succeed, would have to refer to interlanguage as well as native and target language. However, each individual's interlanguage is different and constantly changing, so the task is impossible. Contrastive analysis as advocated in the 1960s was static, whereas language learning is dynamic.

None of this denied the utility of contrastive analysis in designing instructional materials, nor ignored the insights it might yield in studying learners' errors. In fact, contrastive analysis in its "weak version" proved more resilient than its foes had expected and survived to inform many studies in later years. However, it left contrastive analysis with the status of just one of a number of useful techniques, not an indispensable predictive theory. Contrastive analysis has never been shown to be a prerequisite for the creation of valid foreign language tests.

Arising from the new perspectives introduced by Chomsky, research in the 1970s turned toward the discovery of what languages have in common rather than what sets them apart. The focus for study became the common patterns of language acquisition shared by both natives and nonnatives. Evidence began to emerge that all learners have a lot in common (Dato 1970; Ervin-Tripp 1974; Boyd 1975), regardless of their language background. Error analysis, which had always been carried out informally by language teachers and testers (Boldyreff 1930), now attained the status of an entire research methodology. It was established that a great many learning problems arise from irregularities within a language rather than from differences between languages. Learners tend to simplify the language they are learning, often by overgeneralizing from the limited sample to which they have been exposed. Such intralingual errors are fairly inevitable, given the irregularities of the target language itself. Contrastive analysis may account for some interlingual errors, but it will not predict the intralingual errors that arise from the very nature of the target language itself.

The other great principle of testing in the structuralist tradition was that of the discrete point. As has been seen, discrete-point testing in some form or another had been present in foreign language since the 1920s. However, at the early period there was no articulation of a linguistic theory to support it, and often there was little effort to list which discrete points were represented by multiple choices. It was left to structuralist/audiolingual theorists to create an entire theoretical apparatus as rationale for discrete-point testing. As linguists the structuralists had had little interest in semantics. As testers they were not very conscious of meaning. Nevertheless, despite the "scientific" aura that accompanied many discrete-point tests, this form of testing was actually much less logical than its proponents might have wished to think. It would clearly be inane to suppose that a person who knows a set of vocabulary items, be it a hundred, a thousand, or /n/ words, could ipso facto be considered to know a particular language. Starch's vocabulary test in 1916 had been laughed at precisely for making this kind of assertion. However, discrete-point testing assumed that students know a language when they have acquired a finite set of structural items—an assumption no more tenable than the previous one. Moreover, despite the injunctions not to contaminate observations of one skill with another, discrete-point testing never devised procedures for actually isolating discrete points for measurement. Indeed the only time at which a pure discrete-point test could be administered was at the end of students' first day in the foreign language classroom. As proficiency increases, it becomes impossible to test points discretely. In fact, the more the candidate exhibits the construct to be measured, i.e., overall proficiency in the foreign language, the less able is the discrete-point test to measure it by isolating its supposed constituents.

In its search for objectivity, discrete-point testing deliberately cultivated an inflexible mode of scoring. In Lado's words, the best tactic was "to list for the examiner the specific point in the problem which decides whether the response is right or wrong, and to instruct the examiner to disregard everything else" (1964). This was a highly atomistic view of language. Proficiency was gauged on the sum of the elements that were scored as correct, not on how those elements were combined in normal language. It was the examiner who expressed this sum, not the examinee, and this was done arithmetically rather than as an overall judgment. The reductio ad absurdum of these tenets can be seen in Lado's unconsciously ironic statement (1960,160): "We are thus able to break away from having to ask the student to speak when we test his ability to speak, since this process is inaccurate and uneconomical."

The validity of the discrete-point hypothesis could have been supported empirically by studies that would have yielded highly divergent scores on supposedly different language abilities within individual candidates. If language proficiency can truly be subdivided into abilities in different skills, it is obvious that tests of these skills should not intercorrelate well. Theoretically, in fact, if the abilities are truly discrete, they should not intercorrelate at all, though no discrete-point advocate ever adopted this position. On the other hand, if tests of supposedly discrete abilities intercorrelate at a high level, this suggests that a model is inadequate if it views these abilities as separate entities and seeks to isolate them from each other for testing. Rather should they be deemed different manifestations of perhaps a rather small number of underlying factors of proficiency.

Since the first reporting of statistical data on foreign language tests, there has been abundant evidence that separate tests on areas of language such as grammar, vocabulary, listening comprehension, etc., correlate very highly with each other, or, put another way, that they load heavily on a common factor. In fact, Lado himself (1953, 32) reported this at the Georgetown Conference session on testing in 1953, as did Paula Thibault of the Educational Testing Service. Thibault (1953, 28) stated that "everything seems to work equally well in language achievement testing," but blamed the high intercorrelations between different subtests on the crudeness of available statistical techniques. In the 1960s Paquette and Tollinger (1968) calculated that on the MLA Proficiency Tests between .80 and .90 of the variance could be ascribed to one general factor. Myers and Melton (1964), in a study of the MLA Cooperative Tests, found that there was no pattern by which scores on particular subskills correlated better with each other than with scores on different subskills. Upshur (1971) found a higher correlation between an oral communication test and a written composition than between the oral test and a discrete-point speaking test. Rand (1972) and Stubbs and Tucker (1974) produced parallel findings for tests of English as a foreign language, again showing discrete subtests loading heavily on a common factor. In the case of the Test of English as a Foreign Language (TOEFL), Hosley and Meredith (1979) showed that the component subtests all correlated with the total at around .80, a very high figure given the great disparities among the population that takes the TOEFL. Spolsky (Gradman and Spolsky 1975, 69) noted that of all tests published by ETS, foreign language tests yielded the highest internal reliability, suggesting that their constituent parts were tending to measure the same thing. As John Carroll put it (1973, 11):

> We have the paradox that the more we attempt to measure different skills, and the better our measurements of these skills, the higher the correlations among the skills, and thus the more they appear to converge toward the measurement of a single all-embracing skill.

The data were all the more provocative given the imperfect state of the testing art, in which there is an inbuilt tendency for divergence between any two measurements. Error of measurement will always prevent inter-correlations between language tests from approaching too near to 1.00. In this light, the kinds of intercorrelations that are typically produced in language tests demand explication. This is even more so when one makes allowance for the diverse learning backgrounds of those who take language tests, especially the TOEFL.

The tests published by the Modern Language Association in the 1960s did not hold the central stage in language testing for as long as their authors might have hoped. At a conference on language testing held at the University of Michigan in September 1967, a widespread feeling was articulated by Rebecca Valette (1968), who complained that current tests (essentially the MLA tests) "do not fill the measurement needs of the profession." Within a decade of their appearance the MLA tests were falling into disuse. Symptomatic of this lack of interest, the tests were never revised or renormed, nor a second edition published. By the mid-1970s the discrete-point theory had been debunked among testing theorists. Nevertheless, this did not mean that the practice had been universally supplanted. Few data are available on testing practices in high schools or universities in the 1980s and 1990s, but it would be surprising if strong elements of the discrete-point heritage did not persist. Any teacher trained in the 1960s or early 1970s was sure to be exposed to discrete-point testing, and in many the tradition survives. Nevertheless, as the decade of the 1970s progressed, researchers increasingly operated within a construct of proficiency as a global skill. They were no longer striving to smash the mosaic of language; rather, they were seeking ways which might enable the examinee to put all the pieces together.

Though the testing theory and practice connected with audiolingualism had been shown to be inadequate, the contributions of researchers such as Robert Lado, John Carroll, and Paul Pimsleur (1961, 1966) remained monumental. They published a body of material and furnished later researchers with a vocabulary and way of thinking about testing that are still relevant today. The 1960s also brought a spurt in interest in aptitude testing, with John Carroll and Paul Pimsleur publishing tests. In addition, it was the decade of the publication of the first book-length study on testing since the 1920s, Robert Lado's *Language Testing* (1964). A few years later Rebecca Valette's *Modern Language Testing* (1967) appeared, which made Valette the first woman to achieve national stature in foreign language testing.

The 1960s also saw the birth of the TOEFL, surely the single most used and most researched language test ever created. The creation of the TOEFL responded to the need for an instrument to assess the English-language ability of the thousands of foreigners who were beginning to apply for study in U.S. universities. Work in this vein had commenced in the 1930s and had burgeoned especially after the Second World War. These years witnessed a dramatic increase in world interest in learning English, which was mirrored by a rise in international interest in studying in the United States. In 1947 the College Board, in conjunction with the Educational Testing Service, began to publish "English Examinations for Foreign Students," designed to select those whose English was sufficiently advanced to permit them to study in the United States. The examination was normed on over five hundred foreign students in the United States, but details of reliability and validity were not provided. The test measured skills likely to be useful in the scholastic environment, such as silent reading and listening comprehension. Reading was assessed through paragraphs with questions on topics typical of history or social studies courses. Auditory comprehension was tested through the use of a phonograph record: students had to mark multiple-choice responses to paragraphs they heard read on the phonograph. They were permitted only one exposure to the listening passages.

As early as 1946 Robert Lado, working through the University of Michigan's English Language Institute, had published a *Test of Aural Comprehension in English as a Foreign Language*. In 1951 Lado published his *English Test for Foreign Students*. Though important in the history of language testing, because it gave concrete form to Lado's ideas on foreign language testing, this was quite a restricted test, being validated on a mere forty-one cases.

The TOEFL, while not directly a government project, did mark the re-entry of the U.S. government into the field of language testing, because agencies such as the Department of State were prominent in encouraging common approaches to assessment (Spolsky 1990). Indeed, the MLA tests and the TOEFL sprang from the same renewed interest in language testing. In short, foreign language testing in the 1960s reached its highest point since the 1920s.

6

Integrative Language Testing

In opposition to the discrete-point philosophy embodied in the work of Robert Lado and others in the 1960s, interest in the 1970s turned toward the creation of "integrative" tests. The term had been coined as early as 1961 by John Carroll, for whom integrative tests were those that attempted to measure "the total communicative effect of an utterance." Carroll was of the opinion that the integrative approach had several advantages, because it permitted "broader and more diffuse sampling over the total field of linguistic items" (1961, 37). Rather surprisingly, this call for integrative testing by a figure as influential as Carroll met no response for almost a decade. Despite the suggestion for more work on such tests, academic interest in the creation of integrative testing formats in the 1960s did not respond to the faith shown by U.S. government agencies in these formats. Indeed, Valette (1967) and Harris (1969) in their books on language testing made little reference to integrative testing.

It was not until the beginning of the following decade that integrative formats received new attention. Such tests were called "integrative" because they appeared to call upon the examinee to use several modalities at the same time—reading, listening comprehension, syntax, orthography/phonology, morphology, and lexicon—in an active interplay with spoken or written discourse. This marked a significant change in direction from the discrete-point tradition's efforts to compartmentalize the components of language. As Bernard Spolsky put it (1973, 175), "We must try to find some way to get beyond the limitation of testing a sample of surface features, and seek rather to tap underlying competence." Proponents of integrative testing at times had to resort to metaphor to explain what they were trying to create. Eugene Brière used the familiar analogy of the tip of the iceberg in describing the limits of audiolingual testing and what the new testing was trying to get at: "The language tests being used today are limited to measuring what is on the 'surface,' and can give us no information about what is underneath" (1971, 385).

Rose Scheider, a specialist in foreign language testing at the Educational Testing Service, provided what may be the first use of the concept of redundancy in language testing (1962):

> Communications theory has focused upon the role of redundancy in normal speech. The listener usually has several clues to the meaning of an utterance which make it possible to grasp the essential meaning even when large portions of the spoken message are missed for one reason or another. The closer a listener's ability to that of the native speaker, the more clues he will recognize, thus bettering his chances of responding correctly even though he may miss part of what the speaker says.

Later, John Oller attempted to elaborate a language testing theory based on the redundancy of natural language. Natural languages, he pointed out, are systems that use more devices to communicate than are necessary. In Spanish, for instance, *los chicos buenos* signals gender and number three times. In English, *I am* signals first person singular twice. Redundancy permeates languages, and to know a language is in some way to know its redundancies. Rather than being a case of nature's profligacy, redundancy is a vital element of language. It permits comprehension when the medium is imperfect. So we can communicate quite adequately in a crowded room or over a poor telephone line, because redundancy provides enough contextual clues to obviate misunderstanding. In contrast, take a message that contains no redundancy—a telephone number, for example. Here each element or digit contains as much information as any other, and none provides context for the next. If one element is misheard, the entire message is lost; redundancy is sacrificed for economy.

Not only is redundancy essential for comprehension of natural language, but it is central to the speed with which such comprehension is achieved. Competent listeners or readers do not devote the same amount of attention to each single element in a text. They concentrate on some and rely on the redundancy they provide to enable them to almost ignore the rest. A user of language is able to do this because communicative interaction is not arbitrary; it is bound by rules, constituting a kind of law of diminishing returns. In a sequence of communication, every message tends to narrow down the number of possible succeeding messages; within a message, every element tends to limit the form and content of the next. This creates what Oller, borrowing a concept from Carroll (1959), called an "expectancy grammar," the efficiency of which is directly proportionate to proficiency in a language.

The ability to use redundancy to make surmises about uncomprehended elements and predictions about what is to follow was, for Oller and his associates, one of the characteristics of competence in a language. The better one's knowledge of a language, the better is one's knowledge of its redundancy. The greater the redundancy that can be extracted from a particular message, the less information each of its constituent elements has to carry, and thus the greater one's ability to do without any particular element. A construct of language proficiency should therefore, argued Oller in the 1970s, include the capacity to make valid guesses about unknown elements, by using the interplay between the different modes of redundancy employed in the language. In a phrase, one is proficient in a language to the extent that one's utilization of its redundancy is native-like.

The task of the language tester, then, is to devise ways for assessing redundancy use. In the development of integrative testing in the 1970s no format received more attention than that of the cloze test. First used by Taylor (1953) for different purposes, the procedure became the object of sustained study in foreign language testing in the 1970s. The earliest application of the cloze procedure to foreign language testing came with Friedman's dissertation (1964), which reported that the cloze procedure could provide a valid reading test for ESL students. In 1970 Darnell found a correlation of .83 between scores on a cloze test he devised for English and those on the TOEFL.

Subsequently, John Oller authored a large number of studies on the topic and became a principal polemicist in debates on the cloze test in general and aspects of it in particular. To a large extent Oller's studies on the cloze format set the agenda for language testing discussions of the 1970s. His comparisons of scores on cloze tests with results on subsections of general batteries showed the cloze test to correlate better both with the general test and with the individual elements than did any of the subtests. In 1974 Oller and others reported a correlation of .79 between scores on a cloze test they had devised and the TOEFL. Earlier, Oller and Conrad (1971) had calculated a correlation of .88 between scores on a cloze test and those on the UCLA English Placement Examination. In 1974 Stubbs and Tucker reported a correlation of .76 between cloze scores and those on a general examination in English as a foreign language. At the end of the decade, Brown (1980) found correlations of around .90 between cloze tests and the UCLA ESL Placement Examination. Caulfield and Smith (1981) found similar correlations between cloze tests and the MLA Cooperative Examinations.

A number of issues arose out of the study of cloze testing in the 1970s. In itself, the cloze is not a test—it is merely a device for making a test—generally requiring the deletion of a certain number of items from a text, often every fifth or seventh word. The candidates' task is to restore or replace the omitted elements. Many questions of design and scoring were the object of discussion in the literature on cloze testing. Should one insist on the insertion of the author's original word in the text, or should an "acceptable response" be counted as correct? If the latter, how was the acceptability of the response to be established? Ways of arriving at what is to be counted as an acceptable response ranged from the complicated (Darnell 1970) to the simple (Radice 1978). However, it became clear that correlations between scores on the "exact-word" scoring system and those on an "acceptable response" system tended to be very high (Stubbs and Tucker [1974] r = .97; Bialystok and Howard [1979] r = .97).

Limiting the range of responses provided one way of avoiding any problem occasioned by divergence in scoring methods. Bondaruk and others (1975) suggested either giving some letters from deleted items or else providing a jumbled list of all deleted items. A variation of the former procedure would subsequently receive considerable attention as the c-test. Jonz (1976) invented a multiple-choice cloze format. He found that such a test could be scored rapidly and reliably. Similar findings were reported by Pike (1979).

Another important issue was that of the criteria to be adopted when selecting the passage to be used on the test. Mullen (1978) offered evidence in favor of using what she called an "easy" passage, while Alderson (1979) discovered that a more "difficult" passage correlated better with other measures. Of course, such terms in themselves begged questions, because there was no guarantee that testers would be able to judge beforehand which of any two passages would prove easy or difficult. It is really the subjects' performance on the cloze test that answers that question, not any a priori analysis. A theory of cloze testing would suggest that ease and difficulty would have to be defined in terms of the redundancy of the passage as a whole, not on the apparent simplicity of the vocabulary, for example.

A more promising approach to varying the level of difficulty seemed to be to vary the rate of deletion. The generic formula for devising a cloze test is to delete every nth word in a passage. Logically, the lower the value of n, the more redundancy is lost, and thus the harder it is to replace missing elements. Stansfield (1980) found correlation with a general test much higher when n = 9 than when n = 5 on his Spanish cloze passage. The question of distance between blanks was not, however, investigated systematically in the 1970s. Another way of varying the difficulty of a cloze test is to delete items deliberately or "rationally," following some theoretical formulation of what it is the test should measure. In fact, most work with cloze tests in the 1970s continued in the tradition of Taylor, who followed the practice of random deletion, where the value of /n/ automatically selected which and how many words were to be excised.

However, once the test began to be used as a measure of foreign language proficiency, there were grounds for diverging from Taylor's original practice. Brown (1980) and Bachman (1982) both found in favor of rational deletion. It is worth remembering that in Taylor's work with the cloze procedure the focus was on the passage itself, not on individuals' ability to relate to the passage. Since then, random deletion survived in part because of the unwillingness of cloze practitioners to revert to the structuralist strategy of drawing up a taxonomy of elements or analyzing language with a view to setting up some hierarchy of importance. In standard cloze practice, the automatic regularity of the deletion process causes a variety of items to be tested, unrestricted by the subjective decisions of the test maker.

Most findings in favor of cloze testing sprang from work in English as a foreign language, and even in the heyday of its popularity the cloze format never gained widespread acceptance in foreign language teaching and testing. Nevertheless some studies did appear to validate the cloze method for other languages, such as German, Japanese, Russian, and French (Brière and others 1978), Thai and Vietnamese (Oller and others 1972), and Spanish (Stansfield 1980). Hanzeli (1977) reported finding high degrees of reliability and concurrent validity on cloze tests he administered to students of French as a foreign language. A pilot study found the cloze test to be resistant to a practice effect (Kirn 1972), and it seemed to be unaffected by the attitudes of examinees to the topics covered in the testing passages (Doerr 1980). Lapkin and Swain

(1977) claimed that it could give valid results even with quite young children. In support of the integrative nature of the test, it was shown that performance on cloze tests required a global comprehension of the passage as a whole, rather than a dependence on local clues in single words or phrases (Chihara and others 1977).

In sum, there was a fairly widespread belief in the 1970s that tests based upon the cloze procedure provided a simple and economical means of gauging not just reading ability, but even overall proficiency in a foreign language. Nevertheless, cloze tests still did not occupy an unchallenged place in the tester's armory. For one thing, the interplay of the different functions of the constituent variables of the cloze test—scoring method, passage selected, rate, type, and quantity of deletions—was not fully understood. Comparative studies tended to alter only one of these variables at a time and, probably for this reason, did not produce dramatically divergent results. The suspicion remained that simultaneously changing many or all of these variables would provide less satisfactory results (Alderson 1979). Further, it was possible that the ability to do well on cloze tests might be a function of a certain kind of cognitive style, somewhat removed from language proficiency (Stansfield and Hansen 1983).

In the validation of cloze tests John Oller and others attached much weight to the correlations they yielded with such tests as the TOEFL. There was an inconsistency in this, because in the 1970s tests such as the TOEFL still owed a lot to the discrete-point heritage, which cloze theorists rejected. It was, to say the least, unsatisfactory to validate one kind of test against another kind of test to which it was supposed to be superior, a reminder of the problem of validation faced but not solved by language testers half a century earlier.

Some authorities, such as Oller, suggested that the cloze procedure by itself might be cautiously used as a single test of general proficiency, because the correlations it gave with general batteries were so high. However, the exercise provides a very indirect kind of test, and its validity might not be convincing if great importance were attached to the results it provided. A student could be forgiven for doubting that the fruits of years of language study could be properly measured through his filling in a few blanks in a passage. Apart from specifically psychometric issues, there remained the question of the effect that widespread use of such tests might have on language teaching. Even if practice did not foster improvement—and only Kirn's small study (1972) showed that it did not—teachers and students would understandably want to be on the safe side. Extensive classroom practice in cloze exercises constituted a somewhat arid formula for foreign language study.

The other major group of indirect integrative tests to receive attention in the 1970s was based upon applications of dictation as a testing tool. As early as 1913 the Committee on Modern Languages had declared that "the dictation of unseen passages is an excellent criterion of the pupil's ability to understand the spoken language" (Report 1913, 52). Thus dictation has a long history of use in the foreign language classroom (Betz 1917; Leavenworth 1926; Duncan 1950; Stansfield 1985). However, audiolingual theorists judged it to be no more than an inefficient test of spelling:

> Since the word order is given . . . it does not test word order. Since the words are given . . . it does not test vocabulary. It hardly tests the aural perception of the examiner's pronunciation because the words can in many cases be identified by context. (Lado 1964, 34)

Lado's opinion shows a wide contrast with the view of dictation and listening comprehension put forward by later (and earlier) writers on the topic. The description of the dictation process as one of returning what has been given out by the reader is at great variance with the proactive and dynamic view of the dictation task articulated by Oller and others. Proponents of dictation might have argued that, unless Lado's classes were remarkably proficient, a little experience with the exercise must have shown him that a great number of his students were quite unable to "give back" what they had heard; for in dictation the examinees are given neither words nor word order. They are given only the sounds of speech; the rest they must produce themselves. They must discriminate among phonological units, decide on word boundaries, recognize the lexicon, make hypotheses about what they are unsure of, and finally synthesize the result of this analysis into written form. They must perceive, comprehend, organize, and (re)produce in the target language.

Dictation is in this sense a communicative test, for the passage does not consist of a string of unrelated words, but is an organically unified and meaningful sequence of thought. It is the task of the examinees to use the redundancy they can garner from the passage as a whole to solve particular local problems of comprehension. In this respect dictation has much in common with a cloze test. In dictation, the "blanks" are blanks in the examinees' initial comprehension—elements that they do not understand perfectly. They must avail themselves of the context as a whole in order to make valid hypotheses about such blanks. Dictation is akin to a rationally deleted cloze test, where the rationale for deletion is in fact quite a shifting and dynamic one—those elements in the dictation that the students have found most difficult.

Lado's remarks on dictation comprised little more than a dozen lines of his book on language testing. It was perhaps a little presumptuous—even unempirical—of him to so casually sweep aside a tradition that had persisted for centuries. Despite the contemporary climate unpropitious to dictation, an important study on the topic was published by Rebecca Valette in 1964. Challenging audiolingual hostility to the exercise, Valette carried out an experiment that, in her view, showed that for students who had not been specifically coached in taking dictation, "the dictée can validly be substituted for the traditional final examination in first semester French." Valette again supported the general validity of dictation in her 1967 book on foreign language testing, but it was not until the subsequent decade that interest in the procedure spread beyond its traditional bastion in the French classroom.

In 1971 John Oller published his analysis of the role of dictation in the UCLA English Placement Examination. Oller found that scores on the dictation correlated better with each of the other four parts (reading, phonological discrimination, multiple-choice grammar questions, and composition) of the examination than did any other part. It was also the best predictor of the total score. A large number of subsequent studies (Rand 1972; Oller and Streiff 1975; Natalicio 1979) showed high correlations between dictation scores and those on general batteries. It was striking that cloze tests consistently correlated highly with tests of listening comprehension and even more so with dictation (Darnell [1970] r = .73 with listening comprehension; Oller and Conrad [1971] r = .82 with dictation; Oller [1978] "near the .90 level" with dictation). At first glance this was surprising, because there is no aural dimension to the standard cloze procedure. However, when taken in conjunction with the other statistical findings on cloze testing and dictation, the findings led John Oller and others to the belief that tests such as cloze and dictation are capable of drawing a large volume from the well of what they believed to be one common trait of general proficiency.

Valette's original scoring procedure was quite crude, but subsequently she and others evolved more sophisticated systems. Evola and others (1980) discovered that generally with tests such as dictation a scoring mode that credits correct forms appears to be a better indicator of overall ability than one that penalizes errors. Bacheller (1980) sought to establish criteria for scoring based upon the communicative effect of errors in dictation; he reported that somewhat subjective judgments still provided reliable scores. Savignon (1982) continued in this line, contrasting an exact-word scoring method with one that focused on "conveyance of meaning." She found that native speakers of French always scored 100 percent on the conveyance of meaning criterion, but not on the exact-word system. Studies such as these offered the hope of arriving at a rationale for a more sensitive scoring method than merely marking words right or wrong.

Brodkey (1972) found that prior listener experience of the reader's voice allowed higher scores to be attained on dictation. Thus, if dictation were to be used as anything other than a classroom-based test, who should read the passage? Presumably, if a dictation were to be adopted as a crucial part of any nationally administered test, a tape-recorded native speaker's voice would be chosen. However, standardization is unattainable for most languages taught and tested, precisely because they are important world languages. Because even native speakers make errors when exposed to a dialect other than their own, choice of reader could discriminate against some examinees. Of course, this is true of all listening-based tests. Indeed, it is arguable that if the context of the dictation provides a high degree of redundancy, it ought to be less sensitive to dialectal differences than other less integrative tests.

Traditionally associated with French, in the 1970s dictation was widely studied and positively evaluated in the case of English as a Second Language. Its applicability to Spanish was challenged by Stansfield (1981), who found that scores on a dictation correlated poorly with those on a general Spanish placement test. Stansfield thought this to be evidence that Spanish is easier to transcribe than French or English, and that knowledge of the spelling conventions of Spanish was enough to ensure good performance. Stansfield's scoring method—he penalized even minor orthographic errors—may not have been subtle enough for the task he set it, and the passage did not contain enough unfamiliar vocabulary to prove his contention that students needed only an awareness of sound/symbol concordances. Regrettably, this study was not replicated, but the belief that standard dictation does not yield an adequate spread of scores gave rise to experiments with "partial dictation." Johansson (1975, 123-49) rationally deleted those elements in a passage that he deemed most difficult for dictation and provided his examinees with texts in which all but the most "difficult" parts were already filled in.

The test seemed to work well and gave high correlations with other measures. An extreme form of partial dictation was put forward by Aitken (1979). In this "Integrative Grammar Test," the examinee had to write down only a particular word from a dictated text—in this case the second word of a sentence. The sentences were articulated with the contractions of normal speech:

> Whadja do yesterday?
> did

Aitken indicated that a test composed of fifty such sentences correlated with the Michigan English Test at around the .80 mark. Bowen and Plann (1979) judged an experimental integrative grammar test with Spanish not a success, though here the focus was on bilingual speakers. Templeton (1977) designed what he called an "aural cloze," in which every fifteenth word was obscured by a "bleep." All the student had to do was write in the missing word. Results correlated at .91 with teachers' ratings of general proficiency.

It is a grave weakness in the validity of dictation—as it is in the case of the cloze test—that on many passages nonnatives can perform just as well as natives. Gradman and Spolsky (1975) were aware of this. They therefore played background "white noise" during their dictations. The theoretical justification for this was to reduce the redundancy of the passage. Gradman and Spolsky found that scores on this "noise test" correlated well with the TOEFL, and that the test quite neatly divided natives from non-natives. The noise test was supported by Fishman (1980), who added the interesting discovery that when noise was added for the natives, there were "substantial similarities" between the mistakes they made and those made by nonnatives in traditional dictations. However, the validity of the noise test did not recover from the results published by Johansson (1975), who found that a significant minority of examinees became so irritated or tense because of the noise that their performance slumped to the point of compromising the reliability of the test.

Whiteson and Seliger (1975) reported favorably on work with natural background noise, in this case a dictation based upon a conversation in an airplane. Such approaches offered the hope of reducing linguistic redundancy while increasing situational redundancy in a natural communicative setting. After all, for the learner who is incapable of profiting from redundancy a large proportion of foreign language listening consists of mere noise. For him, if he cannot make valid guesses about what is unfamiliar to him, uncomprehended elements are as irrelevant and puzzling as any background hiss or airplane roar. Another variant on dictation came in the form of the repetition test, in which students just had to repeat or reproduce orally what they had heard (Natalicio 1979). Repetition—a kind of oral dictation—seemed to show promise as a testing technique, but has received rather little attention from researchers (Radloff 1990).

In general, then, though a respectable number of validation studies were carried out on dictation, its inability in its standard form to separate natives from nonnatives and its possible susceptibility to a practice effect (Valette 1964) prompted caution in endorsing it as a test of proficiency. In addition, as in the case of cloze testing, its widespread use might have the undesirable pedagogical consequences seen at one time in the French classroom, with students being endlessly coached in dictation taking.

The interest in cloze testing did not wane, but was maintained even into the 1990s. The c-test grew out of the cloze format. As early as 1975 Davies reported on a variation of the cloze test in which parts of missing words were supplied. In the c-test, the second half of every other word in a text is deleted. The text is usually quite short, in order to minimize the effect of cognitive or memory factors and to have as pure a test of language as possible. The c-test also offered the hope of overcoming weaknesses commonly perceived in cloze testing, such as relevance of familiarity/unfamiliarity with the topic.

However, Chapelle and Abraham (1990) found no great difference in reliability between the c-test and other forms of cloze testing. Bradshaw (1990) found that the c-test was rather negatively viewed by those who took it.

One or two other integrative tests received attention in the 1970s. These were more direct than those discussed so far, and their validity was not so directly tied to the concept of redundancy. Among these was translation, or, in its oral manifestation, interpretation. Though perhaps boasting the longest history as a foreign language testing device—"language testing as an academic field is but a recent footnote when set against the history of translation teaching" (Stevenson 1985, 139)—it has been rejected for a long time by many foreign language testers in the United States. Lado (1964) argued that a translation was not a valid test of mastery of a foreign language, only of the ability to translate. This was actually a specious argument, as if one could translate a language without knowing that language. One might have countered with the argument that Lado's discrete-point tests measured not language, but merely the ability to do discrete-point tests. Undoubtedly, had Lado correlated scores on translation tasks with results of other tests, he would have found a very high correlation. It is a little surprising that the task was not rehabilitated more widely in the subsequent antistructuralist theoretical climate. Some sporadic studies, empirical or otherwise (Lococo 1976), were published, but there is no general corpus of research evidence on translation as a testing device.

One of the reasons for this may be quite trivial. Most recent language testing research in the United States, especially that carried out during the boom of the 1970s, has been conducted in ESL. With students from so many different language backgrounds, it is nearly impossible to organize controlled experiments in translation testing. Hence translation has never occupied a place in the testing associated with ESL. However, translation is a highly integrative test, and one that to many, in Europe particularly, seems a fair and natural one. While technical or literary translation may require special skills, the ability to tell what another person just said in a foreign language or to read a passage and tell what it says would seem to offer an intuitively satisfying layman's definition of foreign language ability. Surely someone who purports to know a foreign language should be able to translate or interpret non-specialized samples of it for us. This certainly was the opinion held by those who included the translating/ interpretation task in a test such as the Foreign Service Interview.

The attempt to impose objectivity on the scoring of writing tasks resulted in the borrowing of a device known as the T-unit from the area of rating children's writing in English as a first language. Its creator, Kellogg Hunt, defined the T-unit as "a main clause plus all subordinate clauses and nonclausal structures attached to or embedded in it" (1965). The supporting theory for this form of measurement lay in the concept of "embedding" in transformational grammar. Sentences that have different surface structures may have the same deep structure. The T-unit focuses on the ability to compress ideas or chunks of information into few words. Hunt found that for native speakers the length of T-units increased with maturity: their written language contained more and more results of syntactic transformations. T-unit length increased because the subject improved in ability to control more sophisticated processes of language production. Gaies for English and Monroe (1975) for French found that length of T-units in writing exercises discriminated among learners of second languages at apparently different levels of proficiency. Later Larsen-Freeman (1978) and Sharma (1981) showed that scores that expressed the total number of error-free T-units yielded a more reliable measure. The flurry of interest in the T-unit in the 1970s did not carry forward throughout the next decade, and little research on the topic appears to have been conducted subsequently (Simms and Richgels 1986).

One element to account for the decline in interest in the T-unit in second language may have been the fact that error is much more common in this case and more relevant to the ability to use the language. Hence as a measure of foreign language proficiency some kind of metric of errors had to be built into the T-unit, introducing a complication into what set out to be a straightforward and objective measurement. The measure was really appropriate only for higher levels of proficiency, where the garble produced by density of errors would not count. The T-unit represented a worthwhile effort to marry theoretical linguistics with practical language testing. Indeed, there was no reason why it had to be restricted to the written word; it could just as well be applied to speaking tasks. Even if never validated as a test in its own right, it might offer a means of tracking some kind of index of development for learners—a more meaningful statement of proficiency than descriptions such as "elementary," "intermediate," and "advanced."

Another test that had been ostracized by the structuralists received more attention in the 1970s and 1980s. This was the essay or composition, again a highly integrative test. The focus in this area was on inter-rater reliability, an issue of perennial concern since the 1920s. There were findings that raters could give reliable "subjective" ratings if they were provided a scale on which definitions of each scoring level were spelled out. Kaczmarek (1980) and Flahive and Snow (1980) found that more "objective" measurements of composition, such as those based on the T-unit, were no more reliable in grading compositions than holistic evaluations of communicative effect. This was accepted as support for increased faith in the use of global or "subjective" scoring methods in evaluating written foreign language. Interest in global writing tasks finally percolated through to the TOEFL, which from 1986 on included an essay test of academic writing proficiency. This was scored holistically by trained raters. It still had not been fully integrated into the test, as a candidate's score appeared separately and was not included in the total TOEFL score.

One testing method that has links to the cloze procedure but is substantially different is the reverse-cloze (also called text editing, or cloze-elide). As the name implies, the operation is here carried out in reverse. Instead of deleting words from a text, the test designer takes a text and adds extraneous and irrelevant words. The student's task is to decide which words have been added and do not belong. Fundamentally, the student can make two kinds of errors on this test. He can fail to circle one or more extraneous words, thereby committing what might be termed an error of omission. The maximum number of such errors is the number of extraneous words in the passage. Alternatively, the student can circle words that did in fact appear in the original text, that is, words that are quite correct grammatically and semantically. The maximum number of such errors is theoretically equal to the number of words in the entire passage. Clearly, someone who does not know the language in which a passage is written has no hope of correctly circling extraneous words. Thus, the extent to which one carries out the reverse-cloze task appears to have a relationship with the extent to which one knows the language in which the passage is written. Expressing the hypothesis a little more strongly, the degree to which a person can perform the task reflects how much of the language he or she knows. In other words, success on the reverse-cloze task is a valid index of ability in a language.

The later years of the 1970s saw interest in this test format (Davies 1975; Bowen 1978; Mullen 1979). The latter reported that scores for what she called "non-identifications" (extraneous words missed by the candidate) yielded good correlations with other test scores. Some research on the topic carried out at the Educational Testing Service in Princeton provided evidence that scores on this test correlated very high with other measures, both of reading ability and general language ability such as the TOEFL (Manning 1987). Interest in reverse-cloze testing was slow to permeate foreign language teaching circles, though more recently Blackburn (1993) reported promising work on using the cloze-elide procedure with German and French.

The years of the Vietnam War brought renewed interest in foreign language teaching and testing to U.S. government circles. In 1968 the Interagency Language Roundtable (ILR) was formed, with a view to increasing cooperation in language teaching between such U.S. federal agencies as the Foreign Service Institute (FSI), the CIA, and the Defense Language Institute. A testing subcommittee of the ILR was formed in 1972. A year later the first testing meeting was organized as part of the TESOL convention (Palmer and Spolsky 1975).

Language testing continued to mature in the 1970s. A large body of research literature was published in the main scholarly journals of the ESL and foreign language teaching community. A number of significant conferences on language testing were held. These gave birth to important publications: Clark's "Direct Testing" (1978a) came out of a two-day conference on the FSI test, while Brière and Hinofotis published papers from a 1979 ETS conference under the title "Concepts in Language Testing." Palmer and Groot (1981) published the proceedings of a colloquium at the 1979 TESOL meeting. A Language Assessment Institute was held at the National College of Education in Evanston, Illinois (Seidner 1981). Building on the emergence of language testing as a discipline in the 1960s, researchers in the 1970s now carried out an inquiry whose foundations were built on linguistic theory and buttressed by the incorporation of a new awareness of techniques of statistical analysis.

However, the central debate of the decade, discrete-point versus integrative testing, proved unfruitful in subsequent years. Actually, the instrument most favored by Oller to replace discrete-point testing—the cloze passage—did not differ that much from the fill-in-the-blanks exercise often used in the discrete-point tradition, except that in the cloze procedure much more global context was provided. More significantly, the statistical findings that Oller had used to support his initial claim that language competence was a unitary factor were challenged by theorists such as Vollmer and Sang (1983). Critics were able to show anomalies in Oller's use of factor analysis, especially the use of principal component analysis, which tends to produce a large first factor regardless of the data. Oller had placed too much credence on the strength of this first factor in seeing it as a manifestation of global ability. Oller's theory had also always suffered from an overdependence on statistics and a certain divorce from insights in sociolinguistics. By the early 1980s Oller himself had recognized that his "unitary competence hypothesis" was untenable.

The 1970s saw the arrival of huge numbers of foreign students in the United States. Many of these came from oil-producing states—the Persian Gulf, Iran, Venezuela. These were often subjects in the testing of that decade. In that respect the development of language testing owes something to the oil boom, which brought wealth to countries that had hitherto little tradition of learning English as a foreign language. Allied to this was the increasing use and worldwide spread of the Test of English as a Foreign Language. The TOEFL came to be required by many universities and other U.S. institutions as part of the application procedure for foreigners who wished to study in the United States. The original TOEFL examination consisted of five sections: listening comprehension, English structure, vocabulary, reading comprehension, and writing ability. The examination was revamped in 1976 and reduced to three sections: listening comprehension, structure and written expression, and reading comprehension and vocabulary (Pike 1979). Listening comprehension candidates had to carry out tasks such as selecting the written option that most closely corresponded to a taped statement, and answering questions based on such things as conversations or announcements typical of the American academic milieu.

In the structure and written expression section candidates had to choose words to finish incomplete sentences and identify errors in written texts. In the reading and vocabulary section students had to pick near synonyms in sentences and answer questions on readings. Many hundreds of thousands of candidates in dozens of countries take the TOEFL each year. The TOEFL is undoubtedly the language test upon which most research has been carried out. However, the success of the TOEFL has not had a totally positive effect in testing, because the concentration on testing English as a Second Language to the neglect of theoretical work rooted in the testing of foreign languages has at times produced research dangerously skewed toward one particular language in one particular setting.

The 1970s brought the publication of several new language tests. Perhaps the most prominent of these was the Bilingual Syntax Measure in 1975. This was meant to measure the language development of children by eliciting morphemes commonly omitted by non-natives, such as third person /s/ in the present tense of the English verb. The Bilingual Syntax Measure was the first widely used test that purported to assess Spanish/English oral proficiency of supposedly bilingual children. Children were asked questions based on a series of cartoon drawings. The test was quite widely used into the 1980s. However, it was based upon a very small pilot study, and the test had low reliability. Because it was rooted in syntax, the measure was open to criticism for ignoring other vital aspects of language. Used primarily with children, it became intermeshed with the debate in the 1970s on universal language acquisition stages, that is, the hypothesis that patterns and stages of language acquisition may be similar across languages. Nevertheless, the appearance of the Bilingual Syntax Measure was welcome for its focus on children's learning of another language. It served as a reminder that the great interest in teaching foreign languages in elementary school in the 1960s had produced little of note in the realm of tests designed for use with young children.

Generally the use of sophisticated mathematical techniques that burgeoned in the 1970s seemed to have outrun the sophistication of the theories being offered to analyze their results. The decade gave birth to a new class of professional language testing theorists and experimenters. However, the very expertise in statistics of a cadre of professional language testers brought with it the danger that such testers would become divorced from the classroom. Those whose contributions were most prolific in the form of research articles and conference papers were ipso facto those who were spending the least time in the language classroom.

7

Direct Integrative Testing

Toward the close of the 1940s, Agard and Dunkel had expressed dissatisfaction with the highly pragmatic and contextualized basis of the situation approach as developed by some of the pilot army courses. This opinion was later echoed by Robert Lado (1964). Lado distinguished between what he called the "situations" of language and its "elements." In his view, the situations of language, that is to say the contexts in which it may be used, were infinite. The elements, on the other hand, what would later be termed the discrete points, were finite. Thus, the choice lay between testing a finite number of elements and testing an infinite number of situations. For practical no less than for theoretical reasons, Lado argued that only the elements of language could be validly tested.

To use a more modern formulation of the question, Lado and the structuralists assumed that linguistic competence was a sufficient condition for communicative competence. This opinion was dominant in language testing throughout the 1950s and 1960s. Hence, though they stressed the primacy of speech in the classroom, the teaching and testing practices of the audiolingualists failed to cultivate autonomous communication. The recurring belief that language as used holistically and communicatively could not be reliably assessed had for a long time a stultifying effect on testing practices. In 1970, for instance, Theodore Kalivoda surveyed the oral testing procedures used in foreign language classes in high schools in the Atlanta region of Georgia. He found that the most common tests in use called for the repetition of single words or learned dialogues or pattern drills. Although there was a good deal of ostensibly oral testing being carried out, Kalivoda concluded that it dwelt far too much on memorized material. As he put it, "Only a handful of teachers employed test types which measured expression of thought."

A rather early expression of the belief that this kind of testing was inadequate can be found in a paper by Cooper (1968). Cooper argued for an addition to the traditional discrete-point taxonomy (phonology, morphology, syntax, lexicon). This fifth element Cooper called "context," and he saw it as "a measure of communicative success." Cooper's suggestion was forward-looking, though it was still lodged within the discrete-point mindset. Cooper saw communication as one more discrete element in the test; he never argued that purely linguistic criteria be subordinated to that of communicative success.

It was not until the 1970s that testers began to move totally outside of the discrete-point philosophy. In 1971, John Upshur reported on what he called a "productive communication test." In this, the examinee was presented with sets of four pictures differing in one or two central details. The examiner held identical sets. The task of the examinee was to pick one picture out of the four and describe it in the target language so that the tester knew which one had been picked. Scoring was quite objective; the examinee received credit for the number of pictures the tester correctly identified in two minutes. Success in communication was what counted, irrespective of linguistic accuracy. The scoring system avoided taking a position on the relative importance of form and content, though it did place questionable reliance on the tester as the standard element, in the sense that the burden of the communicative act was not solely on the shoulders of the candidate.

Though work with Upshur's format was not resumed for almost a decade (Palmer 1981), during the 1970s innovative ideas for language testing were produced in the Midwest by researchers such as Renate Schulz, Walter Bartz, and Sandra Savignon. These sought to "devise simulated communication situations in which the student can send or receive an extended message to fulfill a situational task requirement" (Bartz and Schulz 1974). The aim was always to provide maximum contextualization, so at elementary levels visuals or realia were used to elicit speech. In addition, Bartz and Schulz reintroduced the situation task, as in the following example, into academic testing.

Speaking Test

> Pretend that a Spanish student is living with you and will be attending your school for a term. Although his program has been arranged, he would like to know what your daily class schedule is, so that he can get permission to visit some of your classes. Organize your thoughts and give a description of your schedule, including the times of classes, subjects, rooms, and describe the teachers in each case.

For both Bartz and Schulz it was important to test for communication from the very beginning. Tests should relate to the real world, they argued, rather than elicit context-impoverished discrete points. These tests did not seek to separate supposedly different skills such as listening and writing. They allowed for the assessment of both quantity and quality of communication, though both researchers believed that for many purposes a scale measuring quantity of communication alone was sufficient.

This issue, the question of the relationship between quantity and quality in communication, between content and form, is a crucial problem in foreign language testing. Some sources have charged that if teaching and testing methods set success in communication as their goal, linguistic accuracy may deteriorate. The question was posed explicitly in the 1970s, when notions of "communicative competence" were gaining ground. Higgs and Clifford (1981, 61) charged that communicative competence had become a term for communication "in spite of language rather than through language." It seemed to critics such as these that greater value was being attached to sociolinguistic and paralinguistic skills than to ability in the foreign language itself. If successful communication is the only criterion, then incorrect language is just as good as correct language; as long as one got one's message across, full points would have to be allotted even to a student's combination of pidgin speech and energetic gestures.

For some, to be content with such a level of expression was not only a very unambitious goal, but it might, by inducing fossilization of incorrect forms, prevent students from ever progressing beyond garble. It could permit survival in the target language, but would be unlikely to allow normal functioning or integration. And even the question of survival is moot, because real life is not as patient and understanding of errors as is the foreign language teacher.

Some research evidence on this topic was published. Schulz built upon her earlier work to publish an important study in 1977. She found that students who had been exposed to communicative practice performed better on communicative tests than those who had followed a more traditional, structurally based program. However, the latter group performed better on discrete-point tests. This was evidence of a practice effect: the findings suggested that communicative ability could be taught, but that it was not the same as grammatical ability. This position was supported by Joiner (1977), who found that a discrete-point oriented group was inferior to a communicative group on communication tests, but was better on tests that measured "linguistic accuracy." Savignon (1975) presented findings that concurred in part with these: learners who had been given specifically communicative practice performed better than those who had been taught in a fairly typical audiolingual program.

It seemed that communicative ability was not an inevitable by-product of ability to manipulate patterns and structures. In an effort to study how much and what kind of distortion the medium of language can take, researchers in the 1970s increasingly turned to the use of native speakers as judges of foreigners' speech. Guntermann (1978) found that native speakers of Spanish reacted quite "negatively" to some errors, even when it was quite clear to them just what the interlocutor was trying to communicate. In Chastain's study (1980), errors in the imperfect/preterite distinction, so beloved of zealous teachers of Spanish, were among the errors least condemned by native speakers. The error most severely judged by Chastain's group was failure to use an infinitive after a preposition, ironically an unlikely candidate for prolonged attention in the Spanish class. Natives' irritation could hardly have arisen from lack of comprehension of what the foreign students were trying to say. More likely, in Chastain's view, the native speakers were quite intolerant of this error precisely because they believed that the rule it violated was so simple and logical. Thus, ironically, what teachers considered to be the most difficult areas of a language were not actually those areas on which the native speaker made judgments when interacting with foreigners. These insights represented a whole new source of data for the consideration of errors and evaluation.

Despite the newness of the studies with native speakers' reactions to the speech of foreigners, the experiments suffered from the lingering discrete-point tendency to "test one thing at a time," in this case now transmuted into part of a research methodology. Errors were presented in an unnatural context, usually deliberately restricted to one per sentence, with the sentence not forming any chain of discourse. Such a design suited the experimenter, but it hardly reflected how errors really occur. Thus, Piazza (1980) was careful to ensure that in her study the speaker who "made" the errors had "excellent pronunciation," in order to control for everything but the errors that were to be judged. This research design itself created an anomaly, because speakers with excellent pronunciation do not make strings of simple grammatical errors. Indeed, it is quite likely that inferior pronunciation is paradoxically of benefit to elementary speakers, serving as a kind of screen that mitigates the severity of their errors. Wigdorsky for Spanish (1978) and Ensz for French (1982) found this to be so; grammatical errors made with good pronunciation were judged more harshly by native speakers than those made with poor pronunciation.

Most of the experiments with "naive" native raters used students as the raters. However, as Politzer (1978) and Vann, Meyer, and Lirenz (1984) found, factors such as age and educational background have a significant effect on how raters view errors. Other elements that are almost impossible to control are the rater's familiarity with the native language of the speaker, or previous exposure in the rater's own language to speakers of a particular foreign language. These considerations have a heavy bearing on how errors are viewed (Gass and Varonis 1984). An even more crucial variable may be the degree of rater interest in the topic or ideas being expressed by the non-native. If the receptor, for whatever reason, really needs to understand the message, will he not lose sight of the distorted form in which it comes to him? Galloway (1980) found that native speakers were more benignly influenced by the effort to communicate or use paralanguage. Non-natives focused on form, while the natives were interested in content. There are countless other variables that have escaped the attention of testing researchers, such as the physical appearance or personality of the non-native or the degree of motivation or interest on the part of the native interlocutor.

Galloway found some wild discrepancies in the scoring of the native nonteachers in her study. However, other evidence for the reliability of "naive raters" was not so disquieting. Callaway (1977) found that though experienced raters were somewhat more reliable, "both groups are surprisingly reliable on the whole." This is hardly surprising. In daily life we are continually making judgments about how effectively others use language, be they actors, teachers, or politicians. We do not need experts to tell us how to do so. Indeed, it is not even certain that there can be such a thing as an "expert" in this regard, because being an expert in language testing is not at all the same thing as being an expert in language. Why should we not be able to make such judgments about how non-natives use our language? Could "expert" foreign language testers be said to possess a greater command of language than other native speakers of the language? Surely not. If it were countered that they possess a greater knowledge of linguistic and/or testing theory, then the obvious rejoinder is that such information leads away from what the ordinary native speaker brings to the task of evaluating a foreigner's speech. In a narrower, academic context, this belief is reinforced by the heuristic principle adopted in Chomsky's methodology, where the intuitions of native speakers are accepted as scientific data (Chomsky and Halle 1968). Surely, if "naive" speakers can be called upon for evidence as to the acceptability of a first-language utterance, they should be able to make this judgment in the case of a non-native's utterances.

Similarly, the integrated nature of language use in communication argued against the validity of some modern tests. Hence, the Bilingual Syntax Measure (Dulay, Burt, and Hernández-Chávez 1975), in which one element alone in a subject's speech is scored, seemed to offer an inadequate measurement of proficiency. Much the same could be said for the Ilyin Oral Interview (1976), which focused to a large extent on verb morphology. In fact, during the 1970s a number of testers sought to find a place for integrative testing without abandoning the discrete-point heritage. Several writers recommended the continued use of discrete-point tests for elementary levels or as diagnostic aids in designing individualized instruction programs: thus, Valette updated the second edition of her 1967 book of language testing to this effect in 1977. Such an eclectic approach was, however, criticized by John Oller (1976). He condemned what he called the "insidious" discrete-point influence. He believed that this trend operated "on the surreptitious presumption that discrete-point philosophy was actually right all along." Those who wished to compartmentalize the two kinds of tests posited integrative skills as being of a higher order than discrete abilities. However, as Schulz noted (1977), this is by no means inevitably the case: it is not difficult to think of integrative language uses that are less complex than maneuvering discrete points.

Foreign Service Institute Testing

The Foreign Service Institute of the U.S. State Department began to use an oral interview format for the testing of foreign language proficiency around 1956. The original impetus for this came from the National Mobilization and Manpower Act of 1952, which required the Civil Service Commission to develop a register of government employees with foreign language backgrounds. The instrument was designed in specific response to the needs of U.S. foreign affairs agencies. It was felt that if a foreign service officer needed to speak a certain language in the course of his assignment, then his ability to speak had to be tested, not his understanding of the grammar or his production of particular sounds on signal. With this in mind, it was decided to use a testing procedure that would be as close as possible to natural conversation.

The test thus created was called the Foreign Service Institute Oral Interview. The scale upon which oral ability was to be judged ranged from 0 to 5, from "no proficiency" to that of the "educated native speaker." These points were linked to definitions of appropriate performance for each level, based on surveys of the linguistic abilities of working foreign service officers (Thompson 1989). These definitions at first consisted of no more than a sentence in each case, but over the years they were expanded to the point of averaging more than a hundred words for each level except 0. Finer discriminations could be expressed by awarding a + (plus) for each level except level 5.

The interview was generally carried out by two people. Usually one of them was a native speaker of the language in question, and it was he or she who conducted most of the interview. The other, typically a linguist or testing expert, remained mostly a silent partner, though he or she could be called upon to participate in role playing or translation situations. At the end of the interview, the two raters individually awarded a score; if any disagreement could not be ironed out by discussion of the performance, the linguist's score was what counted. To assist the raters in making a rating, a Checklist of Performance Factors was often kept, on which raters entered scores for accent, comprehension, fluency, vocabulary, and grammar. The use of these performance factors grew out of early expressions of dissatisfaction by interview candidates. It was felt that when individuals complained that they had been rated unfairly it was desirable that a breakdown of their performance be available (Sollenberger 1978).

During the 1960s, multiple correlation studies at FSI allowed for a series of weighted values to be attached to particular factor scores. Briefly, this weighting assigned greatest value to the grammar factor and least value to accent. However, the importance to be given to the performance factors diminished as time went by, and indeed policy toward these varied across government agencies. Raters were free to use the factors or not as they saw fit, and in all cases they were subsidiary to the overall global ratings. Outside FSI itself, Hendricks and others (1980), in a factor analysis of results on an FSI-type interview, found that all five performance factors loaded heavily on a common element, casting doubt on whether they could be considered truly discrete, a finding that supported Mullen's study (1977). The performance factors contributed some interesting data in the study of how raters carry out their task. How well did scores on the performance factors correlate with FSI global levels? Clifford (1980) found that the levels assigned by calculating values for the total of the five factors were wrong about one-third of the time. As might be expected, the discrepancy in the great majority of cases was by one FSI level, though in isolated instances the difference was greater. Clifford proposed that this failure of fit was perhaps due to the relevance of skills that were not measured by the performance factors. Sociolinguistic competence, he suggested, might influence overall scores, yet not be tapped by any of the performance factors. Alternatively, he hypothesized that skills were not uniformly relevant to each level; they are "compensatory" or "non-compensatory" at particular levels. So, at level 1 for example, a candidate might show a wide variety of strengths and weaknesses, but at level 4 he had to be good at every-thing. The factor weighting took no account of this.

Adams (1980) confirmed the latter view. She showed that some factors were highly relevant at some levels, but not so at others. Vocabulary, she found, was a vital element at level 0+/1, whereas accent was not. At level 2/2+, fluency was highly relevant, but grammar was not. Slightly further up the scale, grammar became central, and fluency's relevance di-minished. Yorozvya and Oller (1980), on a version of the FSI interview, found that when the separate factors were scored on separate viewings of taped interviews, they showed less intercorrelation than when all factor marks were assigned at one sitting. They argued that there was a halo effect in opera-tion; a rater decided on an overall rating for proficiency and then, perhaps unconsciously, translated this into the discrete performance scores. The statistical studies of the various FSI performance factors showed the tendency for factor analysis to reify unsubstantiated constructs. Very interesting statistics on the performance factors were yielded, yet it was never es-tablished that what was being studied even existed.

In the early 1980s the FSI discarded these performance fac-tors and looked to a new model. Reflecting the current evolu-tion in thinking about language ability, FSI to a lesser or greater extent redefined the existing factors and offered a new set: fluency, comprehension, lexicalization, structural preci-sion, and discourse competence (Crawford, Argoff, and Adams 1983).

In validity, the FSI interview on the face of it surpassed al-most any other kind of testing technique. In order to find out how well a person spoke, he or she was asked to speak; at first glance there was no outside mediation between the ability and the expression of the ability. Inter-rater reliability had been high since the earliest days (Rice 1959). According to Clark (1978b, 26), the two FSI judges agreed to within a + of each other in 95 percent of cases. The figures given by Adams (1978) ranged from 87 percent to 92 percent. When Adams' statistics are broken down to reveal figures for "perfect agreement" and "tolerable disagreement," defined as agreement to within a +, they show that perfect agreement was about three times as likely as tolerable disagreement. The 92 percent agreement, for instance, was composed of 69 percent perfect agreement and 23 percent tolerable disagreement. In another study of rater agreement, Bachman and Palmer (1981) computed inter-rater reliability at .88.

What was the position with regard to less formally trained raters? Many studies used raters who had not been certified or even trained by FSI, but who had familiarized themselves with the scales through studying FSI materials and listening to sample tapes. Henning (1983) cited an inter-rater reliability of .93 on what he called an "improvised FSI interview." Shohamy (1983) reported an inter-rater reliability of .98 among three raters of FSI-type interviews in Hebrew.

Earlier, Graham (1978) cited an inter-rater agreement rate of 93 percent at the Language Training Mission of the Mormon Church in Utah, while Clifford (1978) had shown that oral interview reliability was just as high as on the more "objective" MLA Proficiency Tests.

FSI itself undertook interesting research in this area. Frith (1979) described a restricted but important study in which a group participated in a two-day FSI training session, and afterwards rated a number of sample interviews. They reached an average rate of agreement of 84 percent with trained FSI raters over the first eight interviews they rated, and this subsequently rose to 96 percent. Even more striking was the performance of a parallel group used in the study. These did not attend any training session at FSI, but merely studied an FSI training kit and listened to sample interviews. Rating independently, they too reached a concordance of 84 percent with FSI's own raters over the first eight interviews, and this improved thereafter to 94 percent. These results gave encouragement to the idea of adapting the FSI test to nongovernmental settings.

Thus, there was no shortage of evidence regarding the ability of informally trained raters to operate the FSI scale. Overall, there seemed to be little difference between the reliability figures of these informally trained raters and those of FSI's own specialists. There were, however, a small number of instances of serious disagreement among raters, both formally and informally trained. These exceptions were perhaps somewhat overlooked once the rule of satisfactory agreement had been proven.

Agencies based in the United States such as the Peace Corps and Mormon missionary programs were among the first to adopt the FSI format for their needs. The Peace Corps was not uncritical in its acceptance of the FSI format and by the late 1960s was seeking to modify it. It contracted with the Educational Testing Service to analyze the FSI format and make recommendations for change. This was the first direct contact between ETS and the government testing agencies, one that subsequently was to be often repeated. In a criticism that would echo a decade later, ETS criticized the FSI mechanism for its "relative insensitivity in the lower range of student competence" (1970). It further noticed the narrow range of listening comprehension tested in the FSI format, where listening was essentially restricted to that needed for face-to-face interaction. ETS pointed out that Peace Corps volunteers would likely need skills such as listening to radio broadcasts or telephone conversations, or third-party listening to native-language conversations, with consequent demand for control of indirect speech. Listening, it seemed, was necessary more for a Peace Corps volunteer than for a U.S. diplomat. Among innovations adapted thereafter by the Peace Corps was the procedure of providing students with a list, in English, of points of information that they had to convey in the target language. After the student had made this attempt, the native speaker was asked to recapitulate what he understood the message to be. In a sense this test paralleled Upshur's communication task described earlier.

Given the widespread confidence in the utility of the FSI Oral Interview, it is quite surprising that the test remained for so long outside the mainstream of testing practice in schools and colleges. As has been seen, from the earliest years there was a strong belief in academic circles that oral examinations took too long to administer; indeed, in the discrete-point intellectual environment many doubted the feasibility of rating communicative speech at all. Perhaps the FSI, which operated within a rather introverted milieu and mindset, was not blameless in failing to interlock its testing research with that being conducted in academe.

A number of factors conjoined to provide the climate in which the FSI interview could begin to thrive outside the walls of the State Department. In the 1970s the Foreign Service Institute established a rather close relationship with Georgetown University in Washington, D.C. (Hart-González 1994). This served as an element in bridging the gap between academy and government. In the realm of theory, the decade was marked by a loss of faith in audiolingualism and the failure of any coherent methodology to supplant it. Interest began to shift to the products of language teaching rather than the process. As has been seen earlier, the structuralist model was now shown to be inadequate, and a variety of alternative approaches began to be examined. The late sixties and early seventies had witnessed a popularization of the notion of individualized instruction. Though this never reached a position of dominance in foreign language teaching, it turned attention toward the desirability of setting and defining realistic global objectives for education. The stress on the individual—and what he or she is able to do at any given time—brought with it an interest in criterion-referenced rather than norm-referenced goals. In Europe, a somewhat parallel movement sprang from the need to teach second languages to that continent's millions of immigrant workers. This was termed the "notional/functional syllabus," elaborated with the aim of classifying the different kinds of functional proficiency these "guest workers" would need in their daily lives and work (Van Ek 1976).

On the national level in the United States, domestic and foreign policy played a part in the expansion of interest in testing for proficiency. At home, the decline in the U.S. economy produced an atmosphere in which efficiency and accountability were more stressed than they had been for some time. This was relevant to foreign language teaching, because it was clear that few programs had been operating effectively or producing results in keeping with their costs. Abroad, the rise in importance of new areas of tension served as a reminder that the foreign language proficiency of the American people was inadequate. Indeed, the cultivation of the study of foreign languages and cultures was one of the commitments entered into by the United States when it signed the Helsinki Accords. With these issues in mind, President Carter set up a commission to report on the state of foreign language study in the United States. The commission found that "America's incompetence in foreign languages is nothing short of scandalous, and it is becoming worse." Among a number of recommendations to remedy the malaise, the commission urged that a National Criterion and Assessment Program be set up. This agency "would establish language proficiency achievement goals for the end of each year of study at all levels, with special attention to speaking proficiency" (Report 1980).

Within the academic community, an MLA task force had earlier studied the position of foreign language teaching in universities and colleges. Their first recommendation was "to develop a set of standards whereby achieved proficiency can be demonstrated in ways that are universally accepted and understood, similar perhaps to those used by the Foreign Service Institute" (Report 1978). In academic circles, the growing importance of bilingual education led to demands that supposedly bilingual teachers be asked to prove their ability to operate professionally in a second language. In 1975 New Jersey began to use an FSI-type oral interview format as part of its teacher certification program (Brown 1978). The Canadian province of New Brunswick introduced the test in 1977 with the aim of encouraging its policy of English-French bilingualism (Albert 1978).

The 1970s saw several important conferences devoted to language testing, largely centered on ESL testing. In 1978 a colloquium at the TESOL conference in Mexico City prompted widespread interest. The papers from this session were subsequently published (Brière and Hinofotis 1979). They provide a picture of what issues were of concern in the late 1970s. There are papers on cloze testing and on oral language testing. The problem of validation is also addressed, through both statistical and theoretical avenues. Other significant conferences on language testing were held at Southern Illinois University, beginning in 1977. These owed a lot to the presence at that university of John Oller, and provided him with an opportunity to explore ideas later developed in Oller and Perkins (1980). The 1980 Georgetown University Round Table on Linguistics yielded a forum for testers from the academic world to meet in session with those from government agencies; the papers were published in Frith (1980). Developments such as these paved the way for the dominant movement in foreign language testing in the 1980s, the incorporation of foreign language "proficiency" testing into the U.S. high school and college.

8

The Proficiency Movement

The fact that the academic world paid little or no attention to the testing procedures of the U.S. government for almost a quarter of a century shows the extent to which both worlds—the academy and public service—proved introverted. This paralleled the failure of the most innovative work produced within the Army Specialized Training Program (ASTP) to percolate into the postwar academic world. The initial mechanism for adapting the Foreign Service Institute tradition of testing to the academic environment proved to be the "Common Yardstick" project, a scheme in which the Educational Testing Service cooperated with several European testing agencies to devise a standardized system of measurement for language proficiency (Woodford 1981). In 1981, the American Council on the Teaching of Foreign Languages collaborated with ETS in the creation of a new scale for the measurement of language proficiency. The new scale was in large degree built upon the tradition of the Oral Interview used at the Foreign Service Institute (ACTFL 1982). John Carroll (1967) had found that most language majors at U.S. universities were rated at 2 or 2+ on the FSI scale in their language of concentration. This was held to indicate that about half the FSI scale would be irrelevant at the college level and that the lower points might be insufficiently sensitive to classroom progress.

These findings received some substantiation in a 1979 study at Educational Testing Service, briefly reported by Higgs (1984). In a small-scale and rather informal project, ETS staff conducted oral interviews with thirty high school students.

None was found to reach FSI level 1. Some were 0+, but most rated 0. For Higgs, these findings confirmed the hypothesis that the lower end of the scale did not effectively discriminate and that extra subdivisions were necessary. Weinstein (1975) reported that language majors applying for work with the State Department regularly tested at FSI level 2, unless they had had extensive overseas experience. Freed (1981) found that a sample group of students who had completed French 3 at the University of Pennsylvania scored at an average of 1+, with a range of 0+ to 2+. An ETS study of oral proficiency among first- and second-year high school students showed that none had reached level 1 on the FSI scale, even though their proficiency was considered to span a wide range (Benderson 1983).

It was a little ironic that ETS and FSI should team up in the 1980s, because in 1970 ETS had quite severely criticized the Foreign Service Institute's test. Among several alleged deficiencies, ETS condemned the FSI test for its excessive reliance on face-to-face interaction on abstract topics, and its neglect of important linguistic functions such as indirect speech and asking questions (ETS 1970).

ACTFL's goal in creating the new scale was to offer the possibility of finer discrimination where it was thought needed, while collapsing distinctions at the highest levels of proficiency, those unlikely to be encountered in the academic environment. A somewhat similar rating procedure to that adopted by ACTFL/ETS had been used in the early years of the FSI scale. At that time, FSI raters were empowered to grant minus as well as plus marks throughout the scale. The minuses were later dropped, since it was found that it was not possible to make such fine discriminations (Jones 1979, 105). Though discontinued at FSI, the practice of devising three gradations for a particular level was nevertheless adopted by ACTFL/ETS, who proceeded to subdivide the two lowest rungs of the FSI ladder, levels 0 and 1, into Low, Mid, and High. These were now called "Novice" and "Intermediate" respectively. FSI levels 3, 4, and 5 were collapsed to form one broad band titled "Superior." FSI level 2 was dubbed "Advanced." Operational definitions, averaging about a hundred words, accompanied all of these levels. Unlike the FSI oral interview, the ACTFL/ETS oral proficiency test was designed for use by one tester rather than two and made no overt use of the five "performance factors"—accent, comprehension, fluency, vocabulary, and grammar—long employed at FSI.

The ACTFL/ETS Provisional Guidelines published in 1982 were fivefold, with scales for speaking, listening, reading, writing, and culture. The latter four paralleled the speaking guidelines in their format: operational descriptions of certain kinds of language supposedly typical of the ACTFL/ETS levels Novice, Intermediate, Advanced, and Superior. The culture guidelines were dropped shortly after their publication, and a reworked version of the others was published in 1986. According to Liskin-Gasparro (1987), the new version sought to be less biased toward the commonly taught European languages and attempted to correct ambiguities in the wording of the original provisional scale.

Starting from the first workshop held in February 1982, hundreds of persons were certified to administer the ACTFL/ETS test, and many more acquired an informal familiarity with the procedure. The dissemination of the notion of proficiency and proficiency testing became one of ACTFL's central activities and, indeed, provided a significant source of revenue for that organization. ACTFL designed a program of training in which people could receive certification as officially recognized oral interviewers. This certification process required attendance at a four-day tester workshop, at which participants engaged in a little theoretical discussion and a lot of hands-on practice with sample interviews. In the follow-up phase, which could last many months, the candidate for certification as a tester was obliged to carry out and record a large number of sample interviews. A proportion of these were evaluated by an ACTFL "trainer," whose function was to check on the candidate's elicitation and rating techniques.

In its 1994 professional development program ACTFL listed the cost of the workshops as $575 for members of ACTFL and $750 for nonmembers. For a nonmember from what was termed the "commercial" world the fee was as high as $1,500. A person who wished to attain certification by ACTFL as an oral interviewer would have to pay as much as another $400. Someone who wished to have his proficiency measured by an ACTFL rater would have to pay a fee of $115. A number of other workshops and refreshers were also available geared toward the ACTFL/ETS scale, with the cost for a one-day refresher, for instance, being $175 for a nonmember, and $130 for a member. It was clear that "proficiency" testing was being marketed by ACTFL, providing a significant source of revenue for the organization.

Apart from the training of large numbers of personnel, the ACTFL/ETS guidelines were influential in many areas of the language teaching profession. A large number of foreign language texts, particularly at elementary level, claimed to reflect a proficiency-oriented methodology. There were countless instances of the use of the scale in educational decisions. Hiple and Manley (1987) described how Texas made the attainment of certain proficiency standards obligatory for teacher certification. The state board of education passed a measure that future foreign language teachers should have their oral proficiency assessed "using procedures, criteria, and a passing score in accordance with the ACTFL guidelines." Subsequently state universities such as that in South Carolina required Advanced level for teaching certification candidates. Glisan and Phillips (1988, 529) outlined a Pennsylvania-based program funded by the Department of Education for the preparation of Foreign Language in the Elementary School (FLES) teachers, in which expected language improvement for those who participated in the program was to be defined in terms of the ACTFL scales. The proficiency scales were used by universities as a means of defining entry and exit requirements of their foreign language programs (Arendt, Lange, and Wakefield 1986; Freed 1987). In many states the proficiency movement had a significant impact on curricula and testing at the high school level, with course goals being expounded in terms of points on the ACTFL/ETS scale (Cummins 1987). The New York State foreign language curriculum was drastically revised to reflect a proficiency emphasis, and its venerable Regents examination was redesigned to reflect this. The federal government was prominent in supporting work based on the Foreign Service Institute and ACTFL/ETS procedures. This was especially noticeable in such areas as in the awarding of grants, admission to summer institutes, or qualification for funding (Millman 1988). There were even suggestions that the Oral Proficiency Interview might serve as a national proficiency examination (Magnan 1988, 274).

The ACTFL/ETS scale aroused great hopes among many commentators. For Liskin-Gasparro, a prominent spokesperson for the ACTFL scale, "the value of proficiency tests is that they measure by definition real-life language ability" (1984b, 482). At this very early stage in the development of the ACTFL/ETS test she expressed an equally striking confidence in the guidelines, stating that "although problems still remain, they are logistical rather than theoretical" (1984a, 39). Liskin-Gasparro claimed that the proficiency descriptions were developed empirically, by observing how second-language learners progress. The guidelines, she said, were "descriptive" rather than "prescriptive." In a similar vein, Omaggio (1986, 14) wrote that the scales were "experientially" rather than "theoretically" based, describing how language learners typically function rather than "the way any given theorist thinks learners ought to function."

The widespread support and use of the ACTFL/ETS scale in decisions of importance came in the face of expressions of considerable dissatisfaction with its empirical and theoretical foundations. For one thing, the FSI scale, its concepts and research, tended to be used interchangeably with those of ACTFL/ETS. Empirical evidence for the validity of the Foreign Service Institute test—insofar as it was available to the public—was quoted to prove the validity of ACTFL/ETS, though the two scales differed quite noticeably in their formulations of each level and in the settings for which they were designed. It was a weakness of the FSI Oral Proficiency Interview that it was nurtured in a hothouse atmosphere of U.S. government agencies, where teaching and testing intermesh to a far higher degree than they do outside. The FSI procedure was subjected to few rigorous or skeptical validation studies, especially by external evaluators. Its validity seemed so obvious that it was not studied; in Stevenson's phrase (1981, 38), the oral interview had been "more praised than validated." While the test's validity seemed quite adequate for the restricted use to which it has been put by U.S. government agencies, it was hardly sufficient to go unchallenged if the test were ever to be used in a wider context. Such was the opinion of those who changed the format when creating the Peace Corps test, who expressed the belief that "more delicate and sensitive testing instruments are needed." Ironically, not long after the academic world stumbled across the FSI test, the Foreign Service Institute itself basically discarded the traditional test in favor of a new form of assessment (Bruhn 1989).

The statistical treatment of data by those carrying out research on the ACTFL/ETS scale often begged more questions than it answered. One example of this was the conversion of ACTFL/ETS nonparametric verbal ratings to numerical values for the purposes of computing reliability or validity. Henning (1992) followed Lange and Lowe (1988) in allocating a set of numbers supposedly equivalent to points on the ACTFL/ETS scale. This was done with a view to making scores on the test amenable to numerical analysis. However, there was not an iota of research evidence available to determine whether to assign a value of one or one thousand to a particular level, and just as little to judge how much numerical difference should lie between levels. Indeed, by positing a concocted set of numbers to represent points on the scale, the researchers were actually doing violence to the scale itself, because, as expounded by ACTFL, there was an incalculably greater "distance" between, say, Advanced and Advanced Plus, than between Intermediate Mid and Intermediate High. Lange and Lowe's numbers failed to take this into account and were in fact quite spurious. Intermediate Mid was allotted a value of 1.3, with Intermediate High receiving a value of 1.8. The gap between the two (0.5) was precisely the same as that between Advanced (2.3) and Advanced Plus (2.8), even though the inverted-pyramid model used by ACTFL would demand that the distance between the latter two ratings be much greater. Similar questions were begged by the use of statistics in Stansfield and Kenyon (1992).

ACTFL/ETS failed to publish detailed descriptions of the work and thought that went into the creation of their scales. They also neglected to carry out and publish an analysis of the extensive data base of recordings of its oral interviews, which grew throughout the 1980s. As far as could be seen, little research was conducted on this very interesting body of material. A rigorous investigation of these data by researchers with no preconceived loyalty to the ACTFL scale would have gone a long way toward establishing the validity of many of ACTFL's claims on proficiency. It is ironically true, for example, that much more published material is available about how the examinations of the Modern Foreign Language Study were created sixty years earlier than how the ACTFL/ETS scale was drawn up at the beginning of the 1980s. As can be deduced from the remarks of the test's protagonists, the scale was thrust upon the foreign language community without proper analysis and thought. Some of the claims put forward (Liskin-Gasparro 1984a, 1984b; Higgs 1984) showed merely a modern manifestation of the test makers' traditional hubris—the fallacy that a test always measures what its designers say it measures. Despite the somewhat extraordinary confidence of those associated with the procedure, the new scale initially rested on a tenuous empirical base—a study of thirty high school students. No satisfactory account was provided of such things as how the proficiency descriptions were drawn up, or who decided on the type or duration of training that would be best for those who were to conduct oral interviews.

Similarly, Carroll's 1967 findings provided a very flimsy basis upon which to base the expansion of the lower end of the scale. It would be interesting to count how many times the Carroll study was cited in the "proficiency" literature—certainly cited more often in the second decade after its publication than in the first. This not only evinces an excessive dependence on research carried out decades earlier but prompts the suspicion that many who cited the Carroll study had not read it. For in the Carroll study, apart from a handful that was not counted in the research, no foreign language majors were tested in FSI interviews. The often cited findings by Carroll were drawn up on the basis of quite speculative extrapolations based on statistical correspondences between the FSI test and scores on other tests such as the Modern Language Association Proficiency Exam. These statistics—if statistics they can be called—were just as questionable as those employed in later work on the ACTFL/ETS scale, based as they were on a set of numbers that came out of the researcher's head.

It was, in any case, questionable whether the objective of achieving greater sensitivity had been truly achieved by the changes belatedly prompted by Carroll's findings. ACTFL/ETS now offered six possible levels toward the bottom, as distinct from four on the FSI scale, hardly a dramatic increase in sensitivity. And one of the levels, Novice Low, was defined in terms that described a level of proficiency so minimal that it could be of interest to nobody. The new distinctions achieved a little higher on the new scale, such as that between Intermediate Low and Intermediate Mid, were unlikely to account for any substantial difference in the way a person's proficiency is viewed. It seemed improbable that anyone would post an Intermediate-Mid requirement for a job or as a measure of academic achievement and disqualify those who had attained only Intermediate Low. In other words, it was not clear that the distinction was really meaningful outside the classroom.

If this was the case, it hardly justified the expansion of the lower end of the FSI scale and all the subsequent fuss. It might have been better, rather, to further subdivide ILR level 2 (ACTFL/ETS Advanced). Not only would distinctions at this level of ability be of more interest to those who would use test results, but a subdivision would recognize the fact that, following the inverted-pyramid model favored by ACTFL spokespersons, the "distance" between bottom and top of this level is much greater than that between bottom and top of the Novice level. In other words, if learners could spend years at the Advanced level, why was this only subdivided into two, while the Novice and Intermediate levels had three subdivisions?

The top point on the ACTFL scale was also quite problematic for several reasons. Commenting on the initial efforts to adapt the FSI interview to the academic world, Frink (1982, 282) wrote presciently:

> Although the FSI interview remains the best established test of oral proficiency, it is not necessarily the most readily applicable to high school and college students, even with a modified rating scale. It is based on the premise that the person being interviewed is an adult who will work abroad and assesses ability to function professionally in the target language. Many high school and college students are not yet equipped with any professional vocabulary or with the experience and self-assurance to perform professional-level language tasks.

As Jones (1983, 80) pointed out, research at the Foreign Service Institute was carried out with upper-middle-class adults, "people who could easily strike up a conversation as strangers on an airplane or waiting in a line." In contrast, Jones suspected that using an extended oral interview format with high school students might yield something more like the "deadly" conversations he was accustomed to having with his teenage baby sitters. How applicable, then, was the scale to adolescent students? How much of the scales' progression reflected cognitive growth? There was evidence that the kinds of linguistic operations called for at the high end of the ACTFL/

ETS scale were actually cognitive and developmentally decided (Barnwell 1991). In other words, many of the skills needed to achieve a score of Superior on the ACTFL scale seemed to be abilities that are still in flux as adolescents master their first language. The Superior speaker is supposedly able to "participate effectively in most formal and informal conversations on practical, social, professional and abstract topics and [can] support opinions and hypothesize using nativelike discourse strategies." Even the ability to narrate, supposedly typical not of Superior but of Advanced level, is still in development throughout the teenage years (Nippold 1988, 253-58). An early critic believed that the guidelines "fail to distinguish between general cognitive skills that are independent of the level of proficiency in the target language and language skills that are related to achievement in the target language" (Hummel 1985, 15).

It was thus germane to ask how well adolescents and, indeed, any other speakers would fare on an ACTFL/ETS oral proficiency interview in their own language. Would they score at the highest point, that is, Superior? Unfortunately, there were no published findings on how the proficiency interview handled speakers of any age in their first language. The ACTFL/ETS test set out to measure how non-natives perform, but it never found out how natives perform. (In fairness to ACTFL/ETS, it should be observed that foreign language testing throughout its history has tended to be quite divorced from first-language testing.)

This lacuna was especially troubling in view of the acceptance in the ACTFL training materials of the FSI scale's concept of the "educated native speaker." Pardee Lowe maintained that only a minority of native speakers qualify for the highest ratings: "ILR experience shows that the majority of native speakers of English probably fall at level 3" (1987, 8). If most native speakers score at level 3 (Superior), it must be presumed that some, perhaps many, score below this. And if this is the case for adults, it must be even more so for adolescents.

Another psychometric deficiency in the scale became apparent. Clearly, the persons with whom a speaker has to interact in the target language are the masses of people who have no training in linguistics or language teaching or testing. Because few people voluntarily study a foreign language in order to talk to their teacher, it is safe to say that most learners aspire to communicating with a wide range of speakers outside the classroom and far from the setting in which they have studied the language. This is probably even true of a good number of those American students who take a foreign language as part of a required course of studies (Morello 1988). The assumption that the native speaker is the target of communicative efforts was visible in the ACTFL/ETS Oral Proficiency Guidelines, in both the 1982 and 1986 versions. Though the 1986 scale invoked the native speaker less explicitly, there were still formulations such as "the Advanced level speaker can be understood without difficulty by native interlocutors." Superior level speakers, it was asserted, may make errors "which do not disturb the native speaker."

These declarations came despite the fact that there was nothing near a corpus of knowledge on how speakers of any language react to the imperfect speech of foreign learners of that language, even assuming that the phrase "native speaker" could be meaningfully used without tortuous definition (Paikeday 1987). True, a number of interesting reports on what might be called judgmental strategies followed by native speakers when evaluating the speech of foreigners had appeared by the early 1980s (Ludwig 1982). However, these were far from forming a coherent body of knowledge, and many of them suffered from skewed samples: the raters of foreigners' errors were very often recruited from groups of university or high school students of English, clearly atypical of the general population. Before assertions about hypothetical reactions of native speakers could be validly proffered, a significant set of studies would have to include a wider cross section of raters, including those who would not ordinarily volunteer to take part in psycholinguistic experiments. The more language testing involves native speakers, with all their differing attitudes, prejudices, and idiosyncrasies, the more problematic is the use of any blanket "native speaker" norm (Rifkin and Roberts 1995).

What is the relationship between the ratings made by ACTFL-trained raters and those arrived at by "naive" native speakers? Clark and Clifford (1987, 14) called for more input from native speakers in assessments that used the scale. One study explicitly sought to involve so-called "naive" native speakers in the assessment of performance on the ACTFL/ETS interview. Barnwell (1989) found that a group of Spanish raters in Barcelona who evaluated performance on taped oral interviews of American students were consistently more severe in their positioning of the candidates on the ACTFL/ETS scale than were two ACTFL-trained raters. While this was little more than a pilot study, it served to pose the epistemological question of what it means to be an "expert" in evaluating language proficiency. Were it to be found that native speakers were consistently more strict—or more lax—in their judgments than ACTFL-certified raters, it would certainly put into question the validity of official ACTFL ratings.

Our knowledge of native speakers is at this stage quite inadequate to allow us to predict how they will assess non-native speech, whether they are using a rather elaborate scale such as ACTFL's or merely uttering a binary good/bad judgment. It is a moot question whether any proper generalizations can be made about native speaker reactions and, accordingly, whether a scale can validly cite hypothetical native speaker judgments as indices of a candidate's proficiency. When a scale such as ACTFL's makes references to how the native speaker reacts to speakers of particular levels, it is, in fact, merely offering a set of hypotheses rather than observations from the field.

This problem had been recognized decades earlier by Robert Lado. In 1951 he criticized the invocation of the native speaker as norm in tests developed by innovators such as Walter Kaulfers and Agard and Dunkel. Lado (1951, 532) asked, "What natives are we to take as guides? How can we tell if those particular natives would or would not understand?" ACTFL/ETS made few efforts to arrive at an empirical answer to this question. Indeed, it was striking that, years after the publication of the ACTFL/ETS scale, neither body had as yet published an authorized translation of the scale into the most commonly taught languages. This prompted the question of how the ACTFL/ETS scale could make statements about native speakers when most native speakers of French, German, and Spanish could not even read it in their own language. In fact, by the mid-1990s, the only body to provide rating scales translated into foreign languages was the Peace Corps (Anderson 1993).

Not only did the scale invoke the "native speaker," but the 1986 version complicated matters further by also alluding to putative interactions with "sympathetic interlocutors." Thus, two different norms were used; sympathetic interlocutors are not the same as native speakers. More serious than this psychometric flaw was the fact that the "sympathetic interlocutor" was an even more nebulous term than "native speaker." A native speaker's familiarity with foreigners is something fairly objective and measurable. It is a constant that does not change from candidate to candidate, and one could probably devise some gauge, however complicated, for measuring it if one so wished. A listener's "sympathetic" qualities, on the other hand, are quite unmeasurable on a general scale, because they vary according to the degree of interest in the topic, the physical attractiveness of the interlocutor, whether or not the native speaker is in a hurry or preoccupied with other things, etc. Indeed, a "sympathetic" attitude toward a speaker need not translate into a "sympathetic" attitude to what he or she is trying to say—attitudes toward speech are not identical to attitudes toward the person speaking.

An especially unsatisfactory formulation was the characterization of Intermediate High in the 1986 version, which stated that "the Intermediate High speaker can generally be understood even by interlocutors not accustomed to dealing

with speakers at this level." In other words, the Intermediate
High speaker can be understood even by persons not accustomed to dealing with Intermediate-High speakers. This was
quite circuitous and worthless as a descriptive statement, because it defined Intermediate High by itself. In practice within
ACTFL/ETS usage, the term "sympathetic interlocutor"
seemed no more than a circumlocution for "classroom
teacher," because there are few other non-native interlocutors
likely to be encountered by speakers at the lower levels.

Once the first euphoria had worn off, the ACTFL/ETS
guidelines became the object of sustained criticism. Lantolf
and Frawley (1985) noticed the circuitous reasoning embodied in the scales. Subsequently, they were to call—unsuccess-
fully—for a moratorium on the use of the scale (1988). Others
alleged that the proficiency scale lay too much within the
"discrete-point" testing tradition (Bart 1986; Kramsch 1986).
For critics such as these the scale continued to value grammar
to the neglect of other components of communication. They
believed that a stress on oral proficiency inevitably leads to a
neglect of the many other objectives of foreign language instruction that traditionally provided the rationale for the inclusion of foreign languages in the curriculum. Because only
a small proportion of students, whether in high school or college, would ever have much occasion to exercise their oral
proficiency in the kind of face-to-face interaction tested by
ACTFL/ETS, should the goals of years of activity and study be
expressed in terms of the needs of this minority? If proficiency
was communicative success, could we not look for a richer
definition of communication, one that encompassed such
things as communication with other peoples, through the ability to derive pleasure and benefit from the great achievements
in a foreign language and culture?

Bachman and Savignon (1986) argued that the so-called direct nature of the proficiency test was an illusion—that it was
impossible to divorce a testing method from what it set out to
test. Bachman (1987) later warned of the untenability of oral
proficiency scores were they to be used in hiring or promo-

tion decisions and consequently subject to challenge in the courts. This reflected a general unease at the lack of a sound empirical base for many of the assertions and assumptions of the proficiency movement, as well as dissatisfaction with the haphazard way in which these notions were being disseminated throughout the profession.

Much of the criticism of the ACTFL/ETS guidelines rested on skepticism about the interview format itself (Berrier 1989). In the first place, one of the aims in adapting the FSI test to the academic environment was to provide a shorter interview test; as it turned out, this goal was not achieved. More importantly, the sample of language elicited during an oral proficiency interview tends to be biased in some important respects, favoring certain kinds of language use and penalizing others. In the typical interview, questions by the candidate are far rarer than questions by the interviewer, and are formulistically left to the end as a final hoop to jump through. The interview is quite sterile in the kind of language register or interaction it calls for. It elicits best the kind of coherent, emotionless discourse that is valued in the diplomatic or academic worlds. True, in order to diversify from the inquisitorial mode, role-playing "situations" were employed in the ACTFL interview format, with a view to encouraging certain kinds of language use not easily elicited otherwise. These had an extraordinarily low visual element and were purely word-oriented. The lack of visuals and props in the situation task produced an abstract rather than concrete task.

In any case, to many critics role-playing ability seemed to bring in extralinguistic factors. A candidate has to ad-lib a role he or she has not seen or thought about before—a talent cultivated by actors but by few others (Van Lier 1989, 502). And many native speakers react unfavorably to so-called real-life situations. They provide only short, simple responses, whereas the non-native gets fully into the spirit of the thing and often becomes quite garrulous (Berrier 1989). Lantolf and Frawley (1988, 183) maintained that non-natives, at the Advanced level at any rate, are more verbose than natives. This is not so surprising, because the language for the native is a basic tool of thought and an integral part of his or her culture, while for the non-native it may be no more than a skill to be exhibited. There is always an epistemological tension between communication and testing. Communication implies that one wants to know a person—his or her personality, hopes, attitudes, background and personal history, etc. In testing all one truly wants to know is how well he or she expresses these things.

In this context it was perhaps a pity that more developmental work with the ACTFL/ETS Oral Proficiency Test was not undertaken with ESL students in the United States, instead of confining it to a large extent to U.S. students of foreign languages. Questionable generalizations were formulated based on small samples of Anglophone foreign language students. Generally the proficiency movement was little informed by the ESL testing research of the 1970s. Indeed, the ACTFL/ETS procedure from its inception was already lagging behind that of FSI/ILR, because when the FSI revised the oral interview test in the early 1980s, role playing was abolished (Crawford, Argoff, and Adams 1983).

The task of the candidate in the interview situation is to produce test language, not necessarily authentic language, and the relationship between the two has not been adequately explored. The interview is certainly not a true conversation (Van Lier 1989). In fact, the aim of an oral proficiency interview is to have a good interview, not to have a good conversation. For example, exhibition of what is called "paragraph length" discourse is required to prove Advanced level. This is probably an inheritance from the Foreign Service Institute, where facility with this kind of expression would be valued. However, people rarely speak in paragraphs. In fact, they could not, even if they wanted to. For most purposes, one cannot plan speech like that, because it is interactive and negotiated. At any moment a topic shift can occur. The paragraph is a concept rooted in the world of written language, and to define a particular level of proficiency in terms of exhibition of this kind of language pattern is a value judgment that discriminates against many speakers. The ACTFL/ETS scale associated one level (Advanced) with interpersonal skills, that is, affective and cognitively undemanding, everyday language, and another (Superior) with academic learning and intellectual discourse. It was not coincidental which level placed higher in the hierarchy. Generally, the language favored in the oral interview was what Spolsky (1984, 43) in a slightly different context termed "the variety of academic language chosen as its ideal by the western literate tradition. The style is one that favors autonomous verbalization, that idealizes the communication to relative strangers of the maximum amount of new knowledge using only verbal means."

Adherents of the scale saw these kinds of language performance as discrete levels, rather than viewing them as different manifestations of the same proficiency construct. As Lowe put it (1985, 47), "In everyday life we tend to speak at Level 3, with forays into higher levels as required for technical topics." To this extent the scale paralleled models such as Cummins's Basic Interpersonal Communicative Skills/Cognitive-Academic Language Proficiency dichotomy (1980) or even Bernstein's hypothetical distinctions of "elaborated" and "restricted" codes, first articulated in Britain two decades ago (1971). It also begged the question of why "technical subjects" were to be valued higher than others, and what it meant to make "forays into higher levels." If the native speaker could make such "forays," then perhaps so also could the non-native, given the right circumstances. If Lowe was right to think of speakers going from one level to another, then we should presumably rate speech, not speaker.

Those attending ACTFL training sessions were warned that it is by no means inevitable that all native speakers would rate Superior in their own first language. Some native speakers do not score at this level, it was claimed, because they do not exhibit the linguistic and cognitive patterns supposedly demonstrated by the Superior-level speaker. Factors such as age, socioeconomic status, and regional dialect enter into the evaluation of speech samples and could preclude a speaker from being assigned the Superior rating. Lowe (1987) wrote,

> ENS [Educated Native Speaker] status is normally acquired through long term familiarization with varying kinds of language use from everyday to formal, over a wide number of both abstract and concrete subject areas, and with varying social groups over a period of years from mother's knee into graduate school in America (approximately 21-24 years).

Lowe's remark was not atypical and expressed a view often heard at proficiency testing conferences. It constituted a very problematic understanding of the notion of language proficiency. To say that the majority of native speakers lie at level 3, a full two levels away from the top of the FSI scale, begged the question of what it is that they lacked and what they would have to do to ascend to the top level, that is, 5.

The FSI scale is oriented toward the high degrees of linguistic and cognitive proficiency necessary for functioning as a diplomat abroad. Thus the "educated native speaker" concept undoubtedly has some pragmatic validity in testing the language ability of aspiring ambassadors and embassy secretaries. However, it was accepted in toto within ACTFL circles, and few people within the proficiency movement challenged the validity of such a construct in the teaching and testing of students who have very different needs to those of foreign service officers. Though not always overtly articulated and, in fact, not mentioned in the ACTFL/ETS guidelines, the "educated native speaker" concept underpinned notions of proficiency (Byrnes 1987, 112, Lange 1987, 88). Lowe (1987) pointed to the large repertoire in terms of register and subject area that the educated native speaker can employ. For Byrnes the notion of the educated native speaker was just as relevant to academia as it was to the diplomatic world. Savignon (1985), however, warned against the "elitist" nature of such a criterion, while Valdman (1987) disputed the belief that the educated native speaker really controls a wider variety of language than do others. Lantolf and Frawley (1985) emphasized the difficulty of reaching any homogenous "native speaker" norm, due to the vast differences in register and dialect that can exist under the general rubric of the term. They cited evidence that native speakers may react in ways that would not lead to their attaining a very high oral proficiency rating. Elsewhere (1988) they suggested that in some cases advanced non-natives may use language in ways that are less nativelike than those used by beginners.

Conceived in the hothouse atmosphere of governmental language teaching agencies, the ACTFL/ETS scale was born in an equally restricted environment, the U.S. academy, where the majority of language learners are Anglophone monolinguals of a certain age group. Now undoubtedly a test should reflect the population for which it is designed. There is, of course, nothing wrong with "academic" language testing when the only purpose of language learning is academic. However, the validity of a test that is too deeply rooted in a particular sample of the population must be challenged. The ACTFL/ETS scale was quite introverted in the degree to which it focused on the U.S. high school and university and ignored global language perspectives. This was especially true in the early years of the scale, when it was claimed to have universal validity, across languages and regardless of learning settings, and embodied, in its hierarchical scale, vast claims about the stages through which learners pass.

Given the concept of the "native speaker" as the hypothetical audience for oral interview candidates' efforts to communicate, it seemed that the role of the ACTFL/ETS interviewer/rater was to act as a kind of surrogate for native speakers, eliciting a sample of language used to perform certain communicative functions within particular areas, and making the same kinds of judgments, albeit in a more structured and self-conscious fashion, as do native speakers when they interact with foreign learners of their language. The language sample, if properly chosen and evaluated, ought to predict a wide range of performances with native speakers.

However, the relationship between ACTFL ratings and those made by "naive" native speakers escaped serious study, even comment. There was little consideration, for example, of the amount and type of training administered to ACTFL raters, its concentration on hands-on practices, and neglect of theory. Whatever its merits or demerits, the ACTFL training component represented a process the ordinary native speaker rarely undergoes. ACTFL raters, through a process of shared experience and socialization, learned to use their scale in a particular way. In fact, one could not become an ACTFL certified oral interviewer until and unless one had learned to use the ACTFL/ETS scale in this approved way. Native speakers, in contrast, have no training at all in either eliciting speech or rating it. The operational descriptions for each ACTFL/ETS level are not in themselves self-sufficient or self-explanatory; they can mean different things to different people. The training of interviewers/raters, in which initiates were inducted into a certain interpretation of the scale, provided them with an explication of the proficiency construct that came from ACTFL, not from the world outside. In short, the more formal training given to apprentice raters, the more their experience diverged from that of the native speaker.

In light of the problems associated with reaching an adequate definition of a "native speaker," as well as the extraordinary differences in social class, culture, education, and age that must be subsumed under the "native speaker" rubric, ACTFL/ETS might have done well to hesitate before using this construct in a rating scale. No one at ACTFL/ETS questioned to what extent an academically oriented proficiency tester could constitute a proper stand-in for the men and women in the street with whom the candidate would have to interact in real life. And if not, whose word would count for more in cases of discrepancy, that of the tester or the native speaker? Is a speaker "Advanced" because the rater says so, or is there some reality that is described by the word? There is no evidence in support of the latter possibility.

Did ACTFL/ETS really know enough about native speakers to justifiably invoke them in the scale? The ACTFL scales represent an unsubstantiated prediction of how native speakers would react to certain levels of language proficiency, not a description of how native speakers actually do react. Neither ACTFL nor ETS asked groups of native speakers to perform rating trials with the scale in order to find out to what extent they found the levels a workable way of categorizing foreigners' proficiency in their language. The ACTFL/ETS scale works, if it works at all, as an ad hoc instrument to be used in the homogenous world of Anglo speakers who have learned the language in the classroom. It was far too blunt an instrument to take account of the diversity and richness of speakers, monolingual or bilingual, in the real world.

One of the benefits of research with native speakers is that it reminds us of the danger of becoming insular and inauthentic in the language we teach or test. Because for the most part language teachers and testers share many of the cultural assumptions and experiences of students and testees, they accept and understand things that are quite alien to the native speaker. This was a further way in which the ACTFL/ETS procedure would have benefited from contact with the ESL teaching and testing community, rather than being confined primarily to foreign language educators. The wide experience of ESL teachers in dealing with very disparate student populations was lost because the ACTFL instrument was primarily used with a rather homogenous population of foreign language students. At this stage about the only generalization we can draw from studies with native speakers is that they are more complicated than is implied by the ACTFL scale's easy use of the term.

Not only did the ACTFL/ETS scale set up the native speaker as the criterion the foreign learner should seek to match in speaking ability, but it also set up the putative native as listener or interlocutor. However, the native speaker, who may or may not be an ideal speaker (in a Chomskyan sense), is not ipso facto the ideal listener and is in any case a construct rather than a reality. It is axiomatic that no two people are identical; numerous factors shape a native's reaction to the speech of a foreigner. One of the great tenets of language teaching in the 1980s (and one adopted by ACTFL/ETS in their reading scale) was that it is unwise to speak globally of "reading" ability without reference to the kinds of texts that are to be read. If this is the case, then surely it is equally untenable to conceive of speaking ability without categorizing hypothetical audiences in greater detail. After all, natives differ just as much in oral interaction as do written texts in reading. Buck's description (1991, 68) of listening comprehension as "an inferential process in which listeners construct an interpretation which is meaningful for them" applies to oral communication in general. Hence, a global estimate of oral proficiency for a particular person was ephemeral because a statement of proficiency would have to take into account the context in which that proficiency had been manifested.

ACTFL undertook no field work with bilingual speakers in this country. Strangely, for a test that set out to measure the proficiency of foreign language learners, it was not shown to be appropriate in measuring the proficiency of the millions of Americans who live and work in two languages. The failure of ACTFL to address the question of bilingualism was quite extraordinary, because in bilingualism we find an area in which some kind of uniform, widely accepted, and validated metric would be of immense utility. The millions of bilingual speakers in the United States represent a vast resource which has as yet been but little tapped. At a time when there is a demand for bilingual teachers and social workers, for example, there is an urgent need to establish some means of gauging the extent of individuals' proficiency in the languages they claim to know. A global index of proficiency could also permit meaningful comparison between those who have learned the language in the home environment and those who have learned it as L2 in the classroom. However, the proficiency movement ignored the bilingual speaker throughout the design and implementation of the ACTFL/ETS test. Many U.S.

Hispanics, for instance, have not received all their education in Spanish, hence their opportunities to acquire and practice the academic and intellectual register required for Superior level have been restricted. Though they may speak Spanish in diverse situations at home and at work, they will not always attain the rating of Superior in their own language. It should be quite feasible to use the scale in investigating how U.S. dialectal Spanish is viewed by speakers of the Spanish dialects of other countries.

Foreign language testing research has focused on a truly tiny number of languages. These were the traditional western European core, supplemented from time to time by whatever languages U.S. foreign policy made relevant, such as Vietnamese, Farsi, or Russian. One of the achievements of the proficiency testing movement was the publication of a body of useful theoretical work based on the ACTFL/ETS guidelines but outside the mainstream core of commonly taught languages. This was a model for the kind of work that should have been carried out with speakers of the "commonly taught" languages. The Center for Applied Linguistics (CAL) in Washington (1988) published a Portuguese speaking test that was designed to be scored on the ACTFL/ETS scale, and a similar test was designed for Russian. The Center for Applied Linguistics encouraged researchers to wrestle with the real-world difficulties posed in measuring the proficiency of speakers of languages that are more remote form the western European core (Stansfield and Harman 1987). This work was a relic of the very ambitious goals first propounded for the ACTFL scale in 1982 and 1983, when it was suggested that the scale would have validity across languages, such that an Intermediate High in Chinese, let us say, would be comparable to an Intermediate High in Swahili. One of the benefits that the ACTFL/ETS scale brought to foreign language testing was that to some extent it fostered interest in measuring advanced levels, whereas testing in the discrete-point tradition had tended to focus excessively on beginners.

Interesting issues were addressed in seeking to relate the generic ACTFL/ETS scale to languages far removed from those commonly taught and tested in the United States. There are, of course, many languages that have no "educated native speakers" in the Western use of the phrase. In other languages, if the speakers possess what their culture recognizes as education, it is a long way from the Western academic model. Other languages have native speakers who are educated in the Western academic sense but who were not educated in the language. A native speaker who is educated is not necessarily a speaker who is educated in his or her native language. There are even other languages for which the very speech of the "educated native speaker" is highly atypical of the population as a whole, being marked by such phenomena as code switching or diglossia.

To take one example, those who sought an ACTFL-type scale for a language such as Hindi were faced with the fact that educated speakers of Hindi use English in professional and formal domains. Hindi is used in informal and social settings. Hence the educated native speaker of Hindi rarely gets the opportunity to operate at what ACTFL would call the "higher levels of proficiency." To be a proficient speaker of Hindi one needs to know when not to use Hindi. The case of Arabic also provided some interesting questions as to how to test and rate languages that exhibit patterns of diglossia. Consider also the issues raised by the spread of English as a lingua franca in countries such as India and Nigeria and between speakers from countries such as these. Commentators such as Kachru (1988) pointed out that the internationalization of English made the invocation of any "native speaker" norm problematic. In the future, this may also become the case with Spanish, in the United States at any rate.

Languages and cultures outside the traditional mainstream presented problems of elicitation and appropriateness. Role playing, often employed in an oral proficiency interview, could prove unsuitable for eliciting language from those of other cultures. Even the type of language sought at Superior level, that is, the ability to support opinions and hypothesize, may be hard to elicit in an interview setting in some cultures. For example, a recommended technique for confirming Superior level is to entice the candidate into an argument or vigorous discussion. Nevertheless, according to Loveday (1982), Japanese do not like talking about themselves, nor discussing serious issues with strangers. In many cultures, people consider it rude to argue with a stranger, especially if he has the status of an interviewer or professor. Thus, they will not exhibit the ability to defend opinions demanded for Superior level. If a speaker does, in fact, evince such language use, he or she may for that very reason be linguistically performing at Superior level while sociolinguistically falling below it.

The ACTFL/ETS scale neglected to consider some implications of native speakers' reaction to the speech of foreigners. Native speakers can have very different expectations of a foreigner than they have of each other. There are sporadic suggestions in the literature that native speakers in some cases react negatively to foreigners whose language competence is truly nativelike. Loveday (1982) reported that Japanese native speakers view adversely those foreigners (Caucasians) who speak Japanese well. Those speaking halting Japanese, on the other hand, are praised and flattered. Gannon (1980) has given some corroborating anecdotal impressions from his experience in Canada. Though speaking fluent French, he found that French Canadians appeared to react adversely to him. He speculated that "the target culture may well have a sociolinguistic model or . . . a concept of the correct sociolinguistic behavior for the foreign learner that is different from that expected of native speakers." Gannon asked whether language teachers and testers really know how society reacts to the foreign learner's use of certain types of idiomatic language, for example, or of certain very informal registers of speech. A somewhat parallel finding was discussed by Valdman (1987, 140), who reviewed a study that showed that a group of native speakers of English disapproved of foreigner speech that, though exhibiting a high level of proficiency, bore the influence of regional English dialect.

Hence the invocation of the "native speaker" as the paragon toward which foreigners should strive was more complicated than might first appear. There are very few systematic studies of how society reacts to the foreign learner's use of certain types of idiomatic language, for example, or of very informal registers of speech. Instead of being admired for dominating such modes of expression, it may be that the foreigner somehow breaks a taboo by becoming too colloquial. As Gannon points out, natives have two sets of expectations, one for their fellows and one for non-natives. Each set of speakers has its place. Thus, in the case of the assessment of a non-native's proficiency, rater behavior when faced with the higher levels of proficiency may be less predictable than is assumed by an easy acceptance of the native speaker as the ideal to emulate. In Nichols' phrase (1988, 15), standardized proficiency scaling presupposes "uniform, incremental, and monotonic increases in the ability to speak a language." Such a model may not correspond to the sociolinguistic reality of communication. The curve of natives' positive reactions to increasingly high levels of proficiency does not always climb inexorably upward. It may be that native speakers, in some cultures at least, react most positively to the speech of foreigners whose proficiency is not uncomfortably high. Thus, rather than cleave to the "educated native speaker" norm, perhaps testers should direct their attention to creating some kind of alternative model or abstraction to emulate: the "good foreign language speaker," the "educated non-native speaker," or perhaps even the "ideal bilingual speaker." This question may be amenable to empirical investigation, in the sense that native speakers may, despite their countless idiosyncrasies, share some assumptions about what they value in the speech of a non-native.

At the very least we ought to seek out natives' views on what they think on this and other aspects of proficiency. This implies giving their opinions just as much validity—or perhaps more—as we attach to those of professional language testers. If a person has a view as to someone else's linguistic ability, on what basis can such an opinion be said to be right or wrong? If a professional tester claims that such and such a speaker is poor, and the other judge feels he is good, why should the latter change his mind? What does it mean to "train" a language rater? Does the training invalidate the subsequent ratings?

Though proficiency scales existed for listening, speaking, reading, and writing, the only modality for which an elicitation mechanism was designed was the oral. ACTFL/ETS was unable to come up with any standardized format for measuring listening, reading, or writing. This in itself was something of an anomaly, given the stress that ACTFL placed on the training and certification of oral interviewers. It seemed illogical to place such great emphasis on controlling through certification those who are supposedly trained to elicit and rate oral language, while at the same time having no form of control, indeed, no standardized format to follow for those who are to elicit ability in other modalities. Further, in the oral interview elicitation and rating were inextricably linked. In the other scales, however, ratings could be divorced from any particular elicitation mechanism.

A prominent figure in the "proficiency" movement, June Phillips (1988, 138) admitted that some students do not necessarily have to go through the hierarchical stages posited for reading. She accounted for this by saying that reading is not a natural skill; it is learned. Thus a person could score at Advanced before scoring at Intermediate, making nonsense of the entire scale. Lee and Musumeci (1988) confirmed that the reading levels did not exist as separate hierarchical entities. The listening skill, so often the subject of language testing research especially in the 1970s, received little attention from ACTFL/ETS, though Valdés and others (1988, 421) reported a study that seemed to show that real-life learners do not follow the ACTFL progression in listening comprehension either. It seemed to many that the guidelines truly did describe what Omaggio (1986) had claimed they did not, namely, how theorists thought learners ought to function.

How effective, efficient, and valid was the process of ACTFL training and certification in the preparation of those who would administer the oral proficiency interview? ACTFL tended to project a low level of testing ability on testers not trained by ACTFL. Often what to just about any experienced language teacher would be common sense was couched by ACTFL in pseudo-technical jargon. One instance of this was the "probe," which essentially meant that the interviewer should try to give the candidate a chance to perform as well as he could. On the other hand, the entire ACTFL/ETS procedure, as well as the writings of its proponents, was extraordinarily divorced from the burgeoning field of language acquisition theory of the 1980s. Notions such as "critical period," "monitor model," and "affective factors" were conspicuously absent from the proficiency literature.

Certainly, the issue of inter-rater reliability is always a concern when holistic evaluation procedures such as the oral proficiency interview are used. Magnan's study (1986) found satisfactory correlations among ACTFL-trained personnel rating interviews in French. Barnwell (1987) found that informally trained raters could reach a high degree of concordance in their ratings after a relatively brief period of practice with the ACTFL scale. In this light the cost of the ACTFL/ETS training program seemed excessive, both in terms of time and money. More such evidence was needed, however, particularly as to the kind and degree of training adequate for reaching a base level of inter-rater reliability. Investigations with the FSI scale (Frith 1979; Shohamy 1983) showed that a prolonged period of training did not appear to be necessary for this purpose. In the case of the ACTFL procedure, would inter-rater reliability be compromised by the adoption of a less rigorous training process for those who would use the test? Like certification institutions everywhere, ACTFL proved unwilling to diminish the time and effort needed for certification, preferring instead to insist on a long training period for those wishing to become interviewers/raters. Those seeking certification as ACTFL testers were forced to invest considerable time and money; figures in excess of one thousand dollars were quoted by ACTFL by the mid-1990s. ACTFL justified this by maintaining that the Oral Proficiency Interview (OPI) instrument was difficult to administer. Whatever the validity of that belief in the case of the elicitation component of the interview, there was a fair amount of evidence that a long training period was not necessary for making reliable judgments on proficiency-type interviews (Shohamy 1983; Henning 1983; Kenyon and Stansfield 1993). As one commentator put it, "Assessing communicative effectiveness is not an esoteric skill requiring arduous special training and licensing; it is one of the normal components of linguistic and social adulthood" (Nichols 1988, 14). Nevertheless, there remained untackled questions, for example the relevance of situational factors such as motivation and interest to the reliability of the rater, or the utility of scales and training. As Brown (1995) put it, "Raters appear to have inbuilt perceptions of what is acceptable to them . . . even the explications of the descriptors and the standardization that takes place in a training session cannot remove these differences."

As a practical question, the ACTFL/ETS guidelines were very successful in winning adherents throughout the 1980s and early 1990s, especially among administrators and supervisors. The proficiency movement showed considerable resilience in the face of its critics. Despite a number of attacks from many different angles, the influence of the guidelines remained strong. The agenda for conventions of foreign language teachers reflected the continued influence of the proficiency movement. Whatever the status of the scales with testing theorists and specialists, they continued to remain in the running in foreign language teaching. Decisions were being made on the basis of the guidelines, and this trend showed no sign of decelerating. In fact, it appeared that ACTFL (1992) was pushing for the incorporation of some variation of the proficiency scales into what was termed "national standards for foreign language education." In 1993 ACTFL joined with five other subject matter bodies and the College Board to create a structure to be known as Forum on Standards and Learning in order to address the question of setting standards for learning in the nation's classrooms.

Regardless of the deficiencies of the ACTFL/ETS procedure as a test, it yielded positive effects in the form of worthwhile innovations in textbooks, materials, teacher training, and other areas. However, there was no necessary link between the ACTFL/ETS proficiency test and the focus on communicative language teaching, meaningful language use, and authentic materials that characterized some of the best foreign language teaching of the eighties and nineties. Indeed, parallel practices to these could be found in foreign language teaching in Europe throughout this period, even though the "proficiency" movement was almost unknown there. Language teaching in the United States in the 1970s was already evolving in the direction that the "proficiency" movement later sought to claim as its own. Witness the debate about "communicative competence" that predated the publication of the ACTFL/ETS guidelines. This trend would have been maintained throughout the 1980s, regardless of whether ACTFL/ETS had ever published their scales.

Had the ACTFL/ETS procedure been a drug or domestic appliance, it would soon have been withdrawn from the maket, because its proponents supplied no proof that it did what it claimed to do. It was all development and no research. In the foreign language teaching profession practice has often lagged behind theory; in the case of proficiency, however, perhaps it was the other way around. In 1925 William Balow, in his president's address to the AATS (1926, 31), warned the association's annual meeting that the history of modern language teaching in the United States was full of examples of fads. "However, I believe that most of our fads have been important matters imperfectly understood rather than trivial fancies irrationally urged. Many of our fads have been real ideas newborn, but sent forth to revolutionize the field before they had reached maturity and could realize the modest place they were fit to occupy." Seven decades later, Barlow's observation could be fittingly applied to proficiency testing.

Conclusion

Foreign language testing has now left its American base and stands as one of the most internationally practiced divisions of applied linguistics. Important work in language testing is being carried out throughout the world, from Europe to Australia, and the second century of language testing seems sure to intensify the trend toward such internationalization. This was already manifest in the 1970s, for example, when a considerable contribution to the research on cloze testing was carried out at the American University of Beirut. In later years the Cambridge-TOEFL comparability study (Davidson and Bachman 1990), the study of the relationship of the Australian Second Language Proficiency Ratings (Ingram 1982) to the ACTFL/ETS or ILR procedures, and efforts to bring some coherence to the burgeoning field of language teaching in Europe (Scharer and North 1992) were samples of what might follow. Given the realities of the world economic order, questions arising out of the testing of Japanese (Brown 1995; Okamura 1995; Carpenter, Fujii, and Kataoka 1995) and Arabic (Chalhoub-Deville 1995) were beginning to attract attention.

The early 1990s saw the setting up of the International Language Testing Association and the Association of Language Testers in Europe. Another dimension in the internationalization of testing lay in the growing prominence of great world linguae francae. The case of English was already clear, giving rise to such tests as the Test of English for International Communication (Lowenberg 1989). It appeared possible that at least Spanish and French might follow a similar path toward becoming one of a small number of truly global means of communication. This would prompt the need for instruments to test these languages as they are used in international trade and commerce, diplomacy, and science. India is one of the largest English-speaking countries in the world, and the United States is the fourth largest Spanish-speaking country. Any future history of testing should tackle its topic on a worldwide basis, because it is no longer meaningful to isolate one country. Even small nations such as Finland have been able to produce significant research. On the other hand, vast areas of the world—eastern Europe, Africa, Latin America— have added little to our understanding of language testing. In the long term it is to be expected that these regions will have much to contribute.

Testing as an international activity has been especially strong in the case of ESL, in which discourse on both theory and practice passes easily between continents. The influx of immigrants into such English-speaking countries as Australia and New Zealand spurred interest there in language assessment. In contrast to the United States, where "bilingual" testing has traditionally been oriented to small children, Europe and Australia willingly faced the need to work with large numbers of adult nonacademic learners of a second language. It would seem logical that the United States, still the destination of the greatest number of emigrants, will at some time recognize that the diverse languages spoken by these new arrivals should be seen as a national resource to be exploited rather than as a problem to be eradicated. In the United States bilingual education has more often than not been a misnomer, because its focus was on the English end of the bilingualism, not on fostering maturity in the other language. The United States has never put much effort or money into the testing of people who have learned a second language informally. Nevertheless, these are often very successful language learners.

Foreign language testing in the United States, however, was slow to forge a link with its European counterpart. For example, the government of Spain found progress difficult in arousing American interest in its diploma for speakers of Spanish. Perhaps a little ironically, in spite of the large numbers of American practitioners of the testing art and its history in the United States, the first and only periodical specifically devoted to the topic is published in Britain. The appearance in 1983 of the journal *Language Testing*, originally based at England's University of Reading, was an important landmark in the history of the field. Studies on testing had always received adequate exposure in the professional journals of language teaching though, oddly enough, very rarely in journals of educational measurement or psychometrics. Now for the first time language testing researchers had their own forum specifically and solely devoted to their topic of interest.

The history of any human activity is also the story of the men and women who moved it forward. Many figures have from time to time dominated the field of language testing. Ben Wood and Vivion Henmon did so in the 1920s, Robert Lado towered above all others in the 1950s and 1960s, and John Oller emerged as a figure of fruitful controversy in the 1970s. There were others, too, such as John Carroll, whose association with the field spanned many decades, and Rebecca Valette, the first woman to earn national prominence in the language testing field. In the closing years of the twentieth century such celebrities no longer dominated the debates of U.S. language testing circles. There were instead a large number of researchers, based at universities, government institutes, or testing agencies, working on a disparate body of topics and kept together by a network of conferences and computerized communications.

As happens when disciplines mature, there was an intensification of subspecializations within the field itself. Having reached coherence as an activity in the 1970s and 1980s, foreign language testing research in the United States appeared ready to set out on many divergent paths of inquiry through the late 1990s and beyond. Continued work in the testing of general proficiency was to be expected, as well as further studies of how nonspecialist raters react to and evaluate the speech of foreigners. Given the need for the use of a second language in restricted situations, more work on the testing of language for special purposes seemed assured. Professionally specialized forms of language tests were developing. These aimed to give a "performance assessment" (Brown 1995), an estimate of language proficiency as exhibited in a particular context, just as the FSI rating was rooted in the diplomatic milieu. There was already considerable interest in testing the proficiency in English of foreigners who sought to teach in the United States (Douglas and Selinker 1992).

As the area of performance testing grew, one could envisage proficiency interviews for nurses, lawyers, and persons employed in currency markets or the travel industry. Scores on such tests would have to be validated by job-specific judgments of communication. These evaluations could be made in collaboration with those most familiar with performance, such as supervisors or fellow workers. Were such steps to be implemented, a very large number of people would have to be available to define standards and administer and/or rate interviews. Increasingly, these would be drawn from the general population, that is, from outside the confines of academic and measurement institutions. Indeed, in addition to acting as raters and evaluators, it would be logical for such people to participate in the construction of tests. This would further satisfy the epistemological need to involve native speakers in the elaboration of tests that use them as criteria.

Somewhat parallel to these trends, there was evidence of interest in self-assessment of language ability. This awareness was borrowed from Europe, where self-assessment had been popular since the 1970s (Oskersson 1978). There was no reason why U.S. student involvement in testing should always be limited to the role of testee (Blanche and Morino 1989). Those who devise tests thereby make a prediction about what students will find difficult or easy. However, there is often a daunting divergence between what answers the test writers think an item will elicit and what knowledge the respondents felt was called upon in order to answer. Input from test takers can bridge this gap.

If testing for specific purposes were to expand, it could lead to nontraditional agencies becoming involved in the process. As is true of any language teaching research in the United States, language testing has almost invariably been undertaken by persons attached to the universities or to governmental agencies. The confluence of academy and U.S. government has been quite obvious in the history of foreign language testing from at least the time of the Second World War. Through a good part of the 1970s, language testing researchers were concerned with, in addition to ESL, languages such as Vietnamese or Thai, not commonly taught languages such as French or Spanish. This was of course no accident but represented the trend of federal funding for language testing research. (There is no sign that languages such as Thai and Vietnamese have continued to receive attention from cloze researchers since the end of the Vietnam War era.)

It seems unlikely that the role of the U.S. government in foreign language testing will diminish, but the next century may well also see research in testing sponsored by business corporations, especially those involved in the complex area of international communication, such as telephone companies. Foreign language testing research has actually not been very well funded by nonfederal bodies. For many years there were few examples of approval of testing research proposals either by humanities or science foundations. However, now testing as a business may well move outside of the academy, back to the private sector. The closing decades of the twentieth century have seen a striking decline in the rate of appearance of published tests on the market. This is charted in Buros's *Mental Measurements Yearbook*. The tenth edition of Buros had only two reviews of new foreign language tests; the eleventh had none at all. Nevertheless, in what truly will be a time of instant international communication, the twenty-first century may witness a lively market in the sale of language tests, especially computerized adaptive placement exams.

It was inevitable, too, that the new technologies available in the 1980s and 1990s would be further integrated into the tester's armory. Countless creative uses sprang to mind. The telephone answering machine, for example, could be used in foreign language testing. It was finally a valid and realistic test of language for a human to talk to a machine. Although it took a while for language testers to think of making use of video, it appeared certain that videocassette recorders had much to offer, especially in the area of oral testing (Clark and Hooshmand 1992). The use of video presented at least a partial remedy for the decades-old complaint that face-to-face oral testing takes too long and is very hard to fit into a teacher's schedule. On a more ambitious level, the use of video teleconferencing, which became common in the business world in the 1980s, offered possibilities for formal testing in situations where the cost and effort merited it.

This was also true for the compact disk, whose enormous storage capacity opened up the possibility of truly interactive and individualized testing. Nor could it be long before testers looked to exploiting the international computer network, the Internet. By the mid-1990s it was quite feasible—if still not actually done in practice—for students in a dozen different countries to take a test simultaneously by using the instant access of the Internet. Other procedures for testing at a distance and without the expensive commitment of one professional tester per candidate already existed in the shape of the Center for Applied Linguistics Simulated Oral Proficiency Interview (Stansfield and Kenyon 1992). No longer did testing have to be rooted in one site.

As early as the 1920s testers such as Wood had realized that one of the weaknesses in traditional testing is that a large number of items are "wasted," in the sense that many questions will be either much too easy or too hard for particular candidates. Put another way, the further a particular student is from the norm—be it above or below—the less efficient is a standardized test for that individual. The computerized adaptive tests that began to appear in the 1980s employ items that are tailored to each candidate's level of ability (Larson 1985; Wainer 1990). The computer can monitor which items have been attempted, which of them have been answered right or wrong, and even which wrong responses have been chosen. In thus arriving at an approximate version of the candidate's ability, the computer program can decide which further questions are most appropriate for each individual. All candidates who take the test thus get a fair opportunity and an adequate amount of time to show what they can do—it is in what they do that persons differ.

In this kind of dialog with examinees the computer offers the hope—some might see it as a threat—of replacing expensive human testers by interacting with the candidate in their place and by fine-tuning items. Item response theory, the study of the relationship between responses to test items and the candidate's ability, provides a foundation (Choi 1992). An elaborated theory would offer the hope of specifying such details as how to choose particular items, how to sequence them, based on a candidate's performance or other criteria, and how to judge when sufficient items have been administered. This will place a new focus on the individual test item: because all candidates do not do the same items, a flawed item is unfair for some—those who have to attempt it—but not for others. The computer can also measure the speed at which a candidate answers—a variable that has been neglected in foreign language testing but intuitively seems relevant to a theory of linguistic communication. Rather than dehumanizing testing, the computer offers a way of taking into account individual test taker characteristics, with obvious applications in remediation and prognosis.

There is also the question of the interplay between test items and syllabus. For example, it might be determined that questions that call for the subjunctive are highly efficient in showing a candidate's ability in Spanish. However, that does not mean that a valid Spanish examination would give questions only on the subjunctive, because in most cases the entire syllabus would have to be checked. The weakness of computerized adaptive testing—one common to so many areas of large-scale testing—was that it initially could deal only with a multiple-choice format. Hence it was conservative, and by the 1990s had as yet no way of handling open-ended questions or acknowledging creative or imaginative answers. There remained the risk that the contribution of the computer would go unassimilated, just as decades earlier the language laboratory had contributed little to language testing. Some eight thousand language labs were installed in U.S. educational institutions between 1945 and 1965 (Darian 143). Though they facilitated the implementation of tests such as the MLA test, in the long term the language lab left not much of a mark on testing. The computer's first use in language testing came in the programmed learning and computer-assisted instruction of the late 1960s and early 1970s. The contribution of the computer at this stage was restricted to rather mindless mechanical testing. A little later, the computer acquired new relevance to language testing when it was used to grind out reliability and validity coefficients in the 1970s.

It was evident that the collection of very large data bases of questions and answers, so vital to computerized testing, was restricted to English as a second language, and that foreign languages taught in the United States lagged far behind in this respect. As opposed to the testing of English as a second language, there was little or no recent statistical tradition in the creation and analysis of foreign language testing. No one in foreign languages has ever repeated the range of statistical inquiry of the 1920s. Research questions such as the effects of the length of the test and the time allotted to take it, and the sequence in which items are encountered, had engaged almost no attention among foreign language testers. Throughout the years there has existed the tendency for testing research to become divorced from classroom teachers. The more sophisticated the argument and statistical apparatus that buttress a particular test or testing concept, the more they take language testing away from the domain of language teachers.

A parallel deficiency in language testing remained from the 1920s. Many, if not most, language teachers and institutions that foster language learning claim to do so for reasons beyond purely linguistic proficiency. It is not uncommon to hear language teaching justified in terms of rather tenuous notions of opening students' minds to other cultures, imparting a more sophisticated awareness of the nature of human language itself, and so on. In the earlier years of foreign language testing brave efforts were made to quantify these outcomes. In later years, unfortunately, the profession has shirked these issues. The total failure of the ACTFL/ETS cultural proficiency scale gave proof that language testing is still incapable of measuring some of the hoped-for outcomes of the process of language teaching.

An interesting divergence has occurred as regards the fates of the MLA tests and the TOEFL. Both appeared at around the same time. The former lasted but a few years and never attracted great bodies of research. The latter is still with us today and has become probably the most important language test now in use in the world. It may have been a deficiency in language testing theory—one that arose out of ESL's dominance in research funding—that the TOEFL was analyzed in such detail, without parallel analysis of tests used for foreign languages such as French and Spanish. It is dangerous to build language testing theories based solely on the performance of non-native speakers of English who were considering college study in the United States. A similar kind of overanalysis also occurred in the case of the cloze test. Throughout the 1980s and into the 1990s, interest in the use of the cloze format continued, even though the cloze procedure scarcely responded to the "communicative" spirit of the age in foreign language teaching. The cloze showed extraordinary resilience, evidenced by the volume of work on the procedure being published well into the 1990s (Jonz 1990; Brown 1993; Oller and Jonz 1994; Jafarpur 1995). Generally, the longevity of interest in the cloze test offered evidence that testers still found it much easier to work with the testing of reading than that of speech.

There was, however, little evidence of progress in building on the other testing formats initially supported by John Oller in the 1970s, namely, that of dictation and other "reduced redundancy" tests. Other integrative formats such as translation have for a long time been unpopular in the United States and remain out in the cold. A further hiatus was evident in the area of pronunciation testing, which lagged behind other domains (Major 1987). This exemplified the degree to which foreign language teaching and testing were remote from the masses of native speakers of the languages taught in the classroom. Because teachers and testers were quite accustomed to the classroom dialect of their students—with its Americanized pronunciation of the foreign language—they failed to inquire how native speakers of those languages would react to that pronunciation. The teaching methodologies of the 1990s— such as cooperative learning, in which students interact with each other from an early stage in the target language—favored the emergence of classroom dialects that could very well be incomprehensible to native speakers of the language.

One area that reappeared as a focus for research was that of language aptitude testing. Little progress had been made in this since the 1960s, and the promise of tests such as the Modern Language Aptitude Test had been deceptive (Fiks 1969). Decades later there were renewed efforts to provide predictors of foreign language success (Stevick 1989; Parry and Stansfield 1990; Goodman, Freed, and McManus 1990). Side by side with and as part of work on tests of language aptitude there were investigations of individuals' foreign language learning styles. In the late 1980s the focus in language testing shifted from the macroview represented by the bigger statistical studies of the 1970s to the microview. Interest grew in studying test-taking processes and strategies used by test takers (Grotjahn 1986; Nevo 1989). Emotional variables (Phillips 1992) and cognitive variables began to be seen as relevant to foreign language success (Hansen-Strain 1987; Chapelle and

Green 1992). Individual differences had been pretty much ignored by test designers ever since the 1920s, and it was thus quite belated for test designers to finally focus on the particular person—not population—who takes a test. In so doing language test designers retreated somewhat from their recent predilection for using data gathered from large groups of subjects and subjecting these figures to sometimes tortuous analysis. Indeed, belief in the utility of rating scales may not long survive into the twenty-first century. Rather than witnessing the proliferation of such scales, we may see a movement toward the use of multidimensional and multitasked evaluations or analyses, which provide a more comprehensive picture of an individual's ability than that yielded by any single point on a scale.

For the first time, perhaps, it was noticed that such an apparently simple task as choosing one of several multiple choices may be a process of greater cognitive complexity than was thought. This offered the possibility of studying cross-cultural differences among language takers, an area of inquiry initially opened up by Farhady's work (1979) on cloze testing. Methodology was borrowed from other areas—verbal or "think-aloud" reports, for example—in which test takers attempted to articulate how they operated when taking a test (Buck 1991).

On the theoretical level, it was to be expected that the search would continue for a richer definition of construct validity, one that might subsume the other kinds of validity traditionally listed by test designers (Bachman 1990; Canale and Swain 1980). However, there were further aspects of the current theories of language whose implications for testing had not even been fleshed out by the 1990s. Among these were Universal Grammar, or the claims about the learnability or teachability of language hypotheses (Pienemann 1984). Further, the foreign language methodologies current through the 1980s and beyond—the Natural Approach and Suggestopedia, for example—stressed that learners should progress through a natural sequence of acquiring a foreign language, preferably done in a nonthreatening ambience. The theoretical apparatus constructed by researchers such as Krashen and Terrell—notions like the monitor model, i+1, affective filter, etc.—remained quite unincorporated into language testing research.

A focus that is solely on the theoretical aspect can easily blind us to what is truly going on in the classroom. In the foreign language classroom many, if not most, of the tests used come with the textbook that has been adapted. Hence, in one sense the most influential testers are those who write the test manuals for publishers and provide teachers with entire banks of tests and items to measure the progress and achievement of their students. Especially in the high school, these are the only testers whose work is used by perhaps thousands of teachers and tens of thousands of students. Nevertheless, there is not much evidence that those who are given the task of creating test banks and testing manuals for language texts are drawn from the ranks of those who have been in the forefront of research or debate about testing.

A backwash relationship between testing and teaching is generally taken as being at least intuitively plausible. However, it has never been shown, in the case of foreign languages at any rate, that the form that tests take affects what goes on in the classroom. As early as the 1920s researchers realized that the great majority of teachers worked oblivious to the debates in the professional journals: theory and practice were divorced. During the heyday of audiolingualism's discrete-point and contrastive-analysis tenets, it is certain that many classroom teachers were still committing the "heresy" of using compositions, translations, and dictations as tests and exercises. Decades later, with communicative goals apparently at their apogee, it was evident that many teachers were using non-"communicative" tests. A history of language testing, like a history of any other area of language pedagogy, is confronted with the incomplete nature of its sources. Any discussion of testing that is based on scholarly journals or proceedings at professional conferences is quite incomplete.

To write a full survey of testing one would have to find out what teachers were actually doing in the classroom, what kinds of tests they were using, and how they were grading them. Regrettably, there exist very few sources for this kind of information. Even the many studies that observe foreign language teachers at work in the classroom have by and large ignored how teachers have assessed learning outcomes. This is a great pity, because most tests are ephemeral and have a life history no longer than the time it takes a teacher to return some papers to the class, end a conversation with a student, clean the blackboard, or clear off his desk.

It is rather disquieting when a business whose history spans almost a century has at almost no time in those years reflected on the ethical implications of what it is about. This is the case with language testing. If language testing is an important activity—an impression strengthened by the fact that it has now survived for over a century—it bears responsibilities beyond its own agenda. These include facing the question of whether there are any issues of moral rights and wrongs raised by what language testing does and how it does it. One searches the literature of foreign language testing in vain for signs that this has even occurred to testers. Even within the general social and intellectual antitesting climate of the late 1960s and 1970s—which caused even the College Board to question what it was doing—language testers never appear to have agonized over what obligations they might have to society. A rare exception to this rule had existed much earlier, in the 1930s, when some language testers were conscious that their work had implications for public policy and taxpayers' money. At various times in this century it has been argued that foreign language teaching as carried out at high schools and universities in the United States is a highly wasteful activity when contrasting the large expenditures and great numbers of people involved in it with the tiny number of Americans who emerge speaking a foreign language. There is no reason to believe that the argument could not be made forcefully today. If any global testing instrument were administered to tens of thousands of students today as were some of the tests of the 1920s, it would surely find the same results: most people in our system learn very little of a foreign language, even when ostensibly studying it for years. Foreign language testers thus need to go beyond measuring proficiency and should ask why measured proficiency is so low in the language-learning population.

How effective is language testing, or has it been over the past century? What has a century of testing achieved? Good speakers? Economical methods? Often the real goal of testing is not to find out anything profound but merely to give grades, reward, and punish—to classify, because that is what the educational system needs. The teacher who assigns As, Bs, and Cs at the end of a French 101 college course is not really making any predictions about how his students will handle themselves on the streets of Paris. He is rewarding some and perhaps rebuking those who made little effort. His judgment has no resonance in the world outside. Typically, there is no externally predictive element to the foreign language grade that is assigned; or, if there is, there is an enormous interval between assignment of the grade and exercise of the ability that was supposedly graded.

Contrast this with the need for tests of, say, medical or engineering ability; these must reliably predict how well people will subsequently use that knowledge in building bridges or saving lives. No medical school would survive long if it were unable to stand behind the assurance that its graduates are competent. In contrast, a review of the history of foreign language testing prompts amazement at how little external quality control has been exerted over the decades on the product of language teaching. With few exception, such as the movement toward accountability in the late 1970s, those involved in the teaching of foreign languages rarely have had to face outside scrutiny. In this sense, academic foreign language testing has the luxury of not having to guarantee its verdicts to end users or to affirm what an individual is or is not capable of doing.

A review of the history of foreign language testing in the United States reveals more lateral movement than inexorable forward momentum. Many of the questions posed toward the beginning of this century remain unresolved. However, progress in language testing research can be measured just as well by the kind and number of questions asked as by the number of answers given. Each generation finds new questions to pose; often these questions are never answered, but the very act of posing them is progress.

References

Adams, Marianne. 1978. Measuring foreign language proficiency: A study of agreement among raters. In Clark, *Direct testing of speaking proficiency*, 129-49.

———. 1980. Five co-occurring factors in speaking proficiency. In Frith, *Measuring spoken language proficiency*, 1-6.

Agard, Frederick, and Harold Dunkel. 1948. *An investigation of second-language teaching*. Chicago: Ginn & Company.

Aitken, Kenneth. 1979. Techniques for assessing listening comprehension in second languages. *Audiovisual Language Journal* 17 (3): 175-81.

Alatis, James. 1989. *Language teaching, testing and technology*. Georgetown University Round Table. Washington, DC: Georgetown University Press.

———. 1991. *Linguistics and language pedagogy: The state of the art*. Georgetown University Round Table. Washington, DC: Georgetown University Press.

Albert, Murielle. 1978. Measuring second language speaking ability in New Brunswick's senior high schools. In Clark, *Direct testing of speaking proficiency*, 19-31.

Alderson, J. Charles. 1979. The cloze procedure and proficiency in English as a foreign language. *TESOL Quarterly* 13 (2): 219-27.

Alpern, Hymen. 1933. A modern test in modern literature. *Modern Language Journal* 17: 268-74.

American and Canadian Committees on Modern Languages. 1930. *Studies in modern language teaching*, New York: Macmillan.

American Council on the Teaching of Foreign Languages. 1982, 1986. *ACTFL Proficiency Guidelines*. Hastings-on-Hudson, NY: ACTFL.

———. 1992. *Newsletter* summer/fall. Hastings-on-Hudson, NY: ACTFL.

———. 1993. *Professional development program*. Hastings-on-Hudson, NY: ACTFL.

Anderson, Neil J. 1993. *Manual for classroom testing in Peace Corps second language courses*. Washington, DC: Peace Corps. ERIC EDRS ED 363140.

Angiolillo, Paul. 1947. *Armed Forces foreign language teaching*. New York: Vanni.

Angoff, William, and Amiel Sharon. 1971. A comparison of scores earned on the TOEFL by Native American college students and foreign applicants to U.S. colleges. *TESOL Quarterly* 5: 129-36.

Arendt, J., D. Lange, and R. Wakefield. 1986. Strengthening the language requirement at the University of Minnesota: An initial report. *Foreign Language Annals* 19 (2): 149-56.

Bacheller, Frank. 1980. Communicative effectiveness as predicted by judgments of the severity of learner errors in dictations. In Oller and Perkins, *Research in language testing*, 66-71.

Bachman, Lyle. 1982. The trait structure of cloze test scores. *TESOL Quarterly* 16 (1): 61-70.

———. 1987. Problems in examining the validity of the ACTFL OPI. In Valdman, *Proceedings*, 149-63.

———. 1990a. A comparison of the abilities measured by the Cambridge and ETS EFL test batteries. *Issues in Applied Linguistics* 1: 30-54.

———. 1990b. *Fundamental considerations in language testing*. New York: Oxford University Press.

Bachman, Lyle, and Adrian Palmer. 1981. The construct validation of the FSI Oral Interview. *Language Learning* 31 (1): 67-86.

Bachman, Lyle, and Sandra Savignon. 1986. The evaluation of communicative language proficiency: A critique of the ACTFL oral interview. *Modern Language Journal* 70: 380-90.

Bagster-Collins, E. W. 1930. History of modern language teaching in the United States. In American and Canadian Committees on Modern Languages, *Studies in modern language teaching*, 3-96.

Banathy, Bela. 1962. The Common Concepts foreign language test. *Modern Language Journal* 46: 363-65.

Barlow, William M. 1926. Address of the president. *Hispania* 9: 31-38.

Barnwell, David. 1987. Who is to judge how well others speak?: An experiment with the ACTFL/ETS scale. In *Proceedings of the Eastern States Conference on Linguistics*, 37-45. Columbus: Ohio State University.

———. 1989. "Naive" native speakers and judgments of oral proficiency in Spanish. *Language Testing* 6 (2): 152-63.

———. 1991. Proficiency and the schools. *Hispania* 74: 187-9.

Bart, Benjamin F. 1986. A note on proficiency and communication in language teaching. *ADFL Bulletin* 17 (3): 61-62.

Bartz, Walter H. 1979. *Testing oral communication in the foreign language classroom.* Arlington, VA: Center for Applied Linguistics. ERIC EDRS ED 176590.

Bartz, Walter H., and Renate A. Schulz. 1974. Approaches to the testing of communicative competence. Paper presented at Central States Conference, April, in Milwaukee. ERIC EDRS ED 107108.

Benderson, Albert. 1983. Foreign languages in the schools. Focus, 12. Princeton, NJ: Educational Testing Service.

Bernstein, Basil. 1971. *Class, codes and control.* London: Routledge and Kegan Paul.

Berrier, Astrid. 1989. Evaluation de l'oral: les hauts et les bas de l'entrevue et du jeu de role. *Canadian Modern Language Review* 1: 345-56.

Berttine, W. 1928. Means of predicting success in first year college foreign language work. Master's thesis, University of Southern California.

Betz, Annette. 1917. The function of dictation in the teaching of modern languages. *Modern Language Journal* 2: 150-56.

Bialystok, Ellen, and Joan Howard. 1979. Inferencing as an aspect of cloze test performance. *Working Papers in Linguistics* 17: 26-36.

Blackburn, James. 1993. Reverse-cloze testing in French, German, and Spanish. Paper presented at Carolina TESOL conference, November, in Myrtle Beach, South Carolina.

Blanche, Patrick, and Barbara Morino. 1989. Self-assessment of foreign language skills. *Language Learning* 39 (3): 313-40.

Bondaruk, John, James Child, and E. Tetrault. 1975. Contextual testing. In Jones and Spolsky, *Testing Language Proficiency,* 89-104.

Borg, W. R., and J. S. Goodman. 1956. The development of an individual test of English for foreign students. *Modern Language Journal* 40: 240-44.

Bovée, Arthur. 1925. A suggested score card for attainment in pronunciation. *Modern Language Journal* 10: 15-19.

―――. 1949. The present-day trend in modern language teaching. *Modern Language Journal* 33: 384-91.

Bowen, J. Donald 1978. The identification of irrelevant lexical distractors. *TESL Reporter* 12: 1-3.

Bowen, J. Donald, and Sandra Plann. 1979. Evaluating bilingual competence: an experimental innovative test. In Yorio, Perkins, and Schachter, *TESOL '79,* 178-86.

Bradshaw, Jenny. 1990. Test-takers' reactions to a placement test. *Language Testing* 7 (1): 13-30.

Breed, Frederick S. 1930. The reliability of the Trabue French composition scale. In American and Canadian Committees on Modern Languages, *Studies in modern language teaching*, 187-98.

Brière, Eugene. 1971. Are we really measuring proficiency with our foreign language tests? *Foreign Language Annals* 4 (3): 385-91.

Brière, Eugene, Gerhard Clausing, Donna Senko, and Edward Purcell. 1978. A look at cloze testing across languages and levels. *Modern Language Journal* 62: 23-6.

Brière, Eugene, and Frances Hinofotis. 1979. *Concepts in language testing.* Washington, DC: TESOL.

Brigham, Carl. 1937. The place of research in a testing organization. *School and Society* 46: 756-59.

Brock, Raymond. 1933. An experimental evaluation of various bases for prognosis in Spanish. Master's thesis, University of Southern California.

Brodkey, Dean. 1972. Dictation as a measure of mutual intelligibility. *Language Learning* 22 (2): 203-20.

Brooks, Nelson. 1950. The College Board Achievement Tests in French. *French Review* 24: 141-48.

Broom, Eustace, and Walter Kaulfers. 1927. *A Test of Spanish Vocabulary.* Bloomington, Il: Public School Pubishing Company.

Brown, Anne. 1995. The effect of rater variables in the development of an occupation-specific language performance test. *Language Testing* 12 (1): 1-15.

Brown, James Dean. 1980. Relative merits of four methods for scoring cloze tests. *Modern Language Journal* 64 (3): 311-17.

―――. 1993. What are the characterisitcs of natural cloze tests? *Language Testing* 12 (2): 94-115.

Brown, Richard W. 1978. Oral proficiency testing in New Jersey Bilingual and ESL Teacher Certification. In Clark, *Direct testing of speaking profiency,* 65-74.

Bruhn, Thea C. 1989. "Passages": Life, the universe and language proficiency assessment. In Alatis, *Language teaching, testing, and technology,* 245-54.

Bryan, Miriam. 1966. Tests with a new look and a new purpose: The MLA Cooperative FL tests. Washington, DC: National Education Association. ERIC EDRS ED 012154.

Buchanan, M. A. 1927. *American Council Alpha Spanish Test.* Yonkers, NY: World Book Company.

Buck, Gary. 1991. The testing of listening comprehension: An introspective study. *Language Testing* 8 (1): 67-91.

Buda, Robert. 1931. A French cultural test. Master's thesis. City College, New York.

Buechel, Edwin. 1957. Grades and ratings in language proficiency evaluations. *Modern Language Journal* 41: 41-47.

Burchinal, Mary C. 1916. What should an examination disclose? *Modern Language Journal* 1: 163-71.

Buros, O. K. 1949. *Third mental measurements yearbook*. Highland Park, NJ: Rutgers University Press.

Byrnes, Heidi. 1987. Proficiency: Concepts and developments. *ADFL Bulletin* 18 (1): 9-10.

Callaway, Donn. 1977. Accent and the evaluation of ESL oral proficiency. Occasional papers in linguistics, Southern Illinois University. ERIC EDRS ED 144406.

Canale, Michael, and Merrill Swain. 1980. Theoretical bases of communicative approaches to second language teaching and testing. *Applied Linguistics* 1: 1-47.

Canty, Laura. 1935. Twenty-five case studies of outstanding successes and failures in French classes. Master's thesis, New Jersey State Teachers College, Montclair.

Carpenter, Kathie, Noriko Fujii, and Hiroko Kataoka. 1995. An oral interview procedure for assessing second language abilities in children. *Language Testing* 12 (2): 157-81.

Carroll, John B. 1941. A factor analysis of verbal abilities. *Psychometrika* 6: 279-308.

———. 1961. Fundamental considerations in testing for English language proficiency of foreign students. In *Testing the English proficiency of foreign students*, 30-40. Washington, DC: Center for Applied Linguistics.

———. 1962. *The prediction of success in intensive language training*. Washington, DC: Center for Applied Linguistics. ERIC EDRS ED 038051.

———. 1967. *The foreign language attainment of language majors in the senior year*. Cambridge, MA: Graduate School of Education. ERIC EDRS ED 013343.

———. 1968. The psychology of language testing. In Davies, *Language Testing Symposium*, 46-69.

———. 1973. Foreign language testing: Will the persistent problems persist? Paper presented at ATESOL Conference, June, in Dublin. ERIC EDRS ED 079432.

Caulfield, Joan, and William C. Smith. 1981. The reduced redundancy test and the cloze procedure as measures of global language proficiency. *Modern Language Journal* 65: 54-8.

Center for Applied Linguistics. 1988. *Portuguese Speaking Test.* Washington, DC: Center for Applied Linguistics.

Chalhoub-Deville, Micheline. 1995. Devising oral assessment scales across different tests and rater groups. *Language Testing* 12 (1): 16-33.

Chapelle, Carol, and Robert G. Abraham. 1990. Cloze method: What difference does it make? *Language Testing* 7 (2): 121-46.

Chapelle, Carol, and Pat Green. 1992. Field dependence/independence in SLA research. *Language Learning* 42 (1): 47-83.

Chastain, Kenneth. 1980. Native-speaker reaction to instructor-identified student second language errors. *Modern Language Journal* 64: 210-15.

Cheydleur, Frederic. 1931. The use of placement tests in modern languages at the University of Wisconsin. *Modern Language Journal* 15: 262-80.

Chihara, Tetsuro, John Oller, Kelley Weaver, and Mary Anne Chávez-Oller. 1977. Are cloze items sensitive to constraints across sentences? *Language Learning* 27 (1): 63-73.

Choi, Inn-chull. 1992. *An application of item response theory to language testing.* New York: Peter Lang.

Chomsky, Noam. 1959. Review of *Verbal behaviour*, by B. F. Skinner. *Language* 35 (1): 26-58.

Chomsky, Noam, and Morris Halle. 1968. *The sound pattern of English.* New York: Harper and Row.

Clark, John L. D. 1965. MLA Cooperative Foreign Language Tests. *Journal of Educational Measurement* 2 (2): 234-44.

————. 1978a. *Direct testing of speaking proficiency: Theory and application.* Princeton: Educational Testing Service.

————. 1978b. Psychometric considerations in language testing. In Spolsky, *Approaches to language testing,* 15-30.

————. 1988. Validation of a tape-mediated ACTFL/ILR scale based test of Chinese speaking ability. *Language Testing* 5 (2): 187-205.

Clark, John L. D., and Ray Clifford. 1987. The FSI/ILR/ACTFL proficiency scales and testing techniques: Development, current status, and needed research. In Valdman, *Proceedings,* 1-18.

Clark, John L. D., and Dariush Hooshmand. 1992. "Screen-to-screen" testing: An exploratory study of oral proficiency interviewing using video teleconferencing. *System* 20: 293-304.

Clarke, Frances Marguerite. 1931. Results of the Bryn Mawr test in French administered in New York City high schools. *Bulletin of High Points* 13 (2): 4-13.

Clifford, Ray. 1978. Reliability and validity of language aspects contributing to oral proficiency of prospective teachers of German. In Clark, *Direct testing of speaking proficiency*, 193-210.

———. 1980. Foreign Service Institute factor scores and global ratings. In Frith, *Measuring spoken language proficiency*, 27-30.

Coleman, Algernon. 1929. *The teaching of modern languages in the United States*. Chicago: University of Chicago Press.

College Entrance Examination Board. 1918. Eighteenth annual report. New York.

———. 1932. Thirty-second annual report. New York.

———. 1941. *Description of examination subjects*. Princeton: Educational Testing Service.

Cooper, Robert L. 1968. An elaborated language testing model. *Language Learning*, special issue, no. 3: 57-72.

Crawford, Gary, H. David Argoff, and Marianne Adams. 1983. *Oral language proficiency testing at the Foreign Service Institute*. Washington, D.C: Foreign Service Institute.

Cummins, Jim 1980. The entry/exit fallacy in bilingual education. *NABE Journal* 4 (3): 25-59.

Cummins, Patricia. 1987. School-college articulation and proficiency standards: a status report. *ADFL Bulletin* 19: 8-15.

Darian, Steven G. 1972. *English as a foreign language: History, background and methods of teaching*. Norman: University of Oklahoma Press.

Darnell, Donald K. 1970. Clozentropy: A procedure for testing English language proficiency of foreign students. *Speech Monographs* 37 (1): 36-46.

Davidson, Fred, and Lyle Bachman. 1990. The Cambridge-TOEFL comparability study. In Standardization in language testing, ed. John de Jong. *AILA Review*, Amsterdam. 7: 24-45.

Davies, Alan, ed. 1968. Language testing symposium. London: Oxford University Press.

———. 1975. Two tests of speeded reading. In Jones and Spolsky, *Testing language proficiency*, 119-30.

Decker, W. C. 1925. Oral and aural tests as integral parts of the Regents examination. *Modern Language Journal* 10: 369-71.

Doerr, Naomi. 1980. The effects of agreement/disagreement upon cloze scores. In Oller and Perkins, *Research in language testing*, 134-41.

Downey, Matthew T. 1965. *Ben D. Wood: Educational reformer.* Princeton: Educational Testing Service.

Dulay, Heidi, Marina Burt, and Eduardo Hernández-Chávez. 1975. *Bilingual syntax measure.* New York: Harcourt Brace Jovanovich.

Duncan, Maude Helen. 1950. Dictation in the modern language class. *French Review* 23: 393-96.

Dyer, Henry S. 1964. The College Board Achievement Tests. *College Board Review,* no. 54: 6-8.

Eddy, Helen. 1930. Review of *Teaching of modern languages,* by Algernon Coleman. *French Review* 3 (3): 282-84.

Educational Testing Service. 1970. *Proposal for the development of a language testing program for the Peace Corps.* Princeton: Educational Testing Service. ERIC EDRS ED 043024.

Ensz, Kathleen. 1982. French attitudes towards speech errors. *Modern Language Journal* 66: 133-39.

Espinosa, Aurelio. 1927. *Stanford Spanish Test.* Stanford: Stanford University Press.

Evans, Marjorie. 1937. The measurement of French pronunciation. Master's thesis, Ohio State University.

Farhady, Hossein. 1979. The disjunctive fallacy between discrete-point and integrative tests. *TESOL Quarterly* 13 (3): 347-57.

Feder, Daniel, and Grace Cochran. 1936. Comprehension maturity tests: A new departure in measuring reading ability. *Modern Language Journal* 20: 201-208.

Ferguson, Charles. 1966. Applied linguistics. In *Reports of the Northeast Conference,* ed. Robert Mead, 50-58. Manasha, Wisconsin: George Banta.

Ficken, Clarence. 1937. Intercorrelations of part scores in foreign language tests. Ph.D diss., University of Wisconsin.

Fife, Robert. 1928. Trends in modern language teaching. *French Review* 1 (2): 5-17.

————. 1931. *Summary of reports on the modern foreign languages.* New York: Macmillan.

Fiks, A. I. 1968. *The Modern Language Aptitude Test in a Peace Corps context.* Washington, DC: Peace Corps. ERIC EDRS ED 050136.

Flahive, Douglas, and Becky Snow. 1980. Measures of syntactic complexity in evaluating ESL composition. In Oller and Perkins, *Research in language testing,* 171-76.

Fleagle, Frederick. 1923. Modern language tests in North Carolina. *Modern Language Journal* 8: 179-81.

Freed, Barbara. 1981. Establishing proficiency-based language requirements. *ADFL Bulletin* 13 (2): 6-12.

————. 1987. Preliminary impressions of the effects of proficiency-based language requirements. *Foreign Language Annals* 20 (2): 139-46.

Friedman, M. M. 1964. The use of the cloze procedure for improving the reading comprehension of foreign students at the University of Florida. Ph.D diss., University of Florida.

Frink, Helen. 1982. Oral testing for first-year language classes. *Foreign Language Annals* 14 (4): 281-87.

Frith, James R. 1979. Testing the FSI testing kit. *ADFL Bulletin* 11 (2): 12-14.

————, ed. 1980. *Measuring spoken language proficiency.* Washington, DC: Georgetown University Press.

Frizzle, A. L. 1950. *A study of the influence of the Regents Examination in French.* New York: Teachers College.

Fuchs, Gustave. 1932. Standards and practices in administering the modern language requirement for the degree of doctor of philosophy. Ph.D diss., University of Nebraska.

Furness, Edna. 1952. An experiment in objective measurement of aural comprehension in Spanish. Ph.D diss., University of Colorado.

Gaies, Stephen. 1980. T-Unit analysis in second language research. *TESOL Quarterly* 14 (1) :53-60.

Galloway, Vicky. 1980. Perceptions of the communicative efforts of American students of Spanish. *Modern Language Journal* 64: 428-33.

Gannon, R. E. 1980. Appropriateness and the foreign language learner. *English Language Teaching Journal* 34: 90-93.

Gass, Susan, and Evangeline Varonis. 1984. The effect of familiarity on the comprehensibility of nonnative speech. *Language Learning* 34 (1): 65-90.

Geiger, Karola. 1940. A method of checking outside reading. *French Review* 14: 138-41.

Ghigo, Francis. 1943. Standardized Tests in the ASTP at the University of North Carolina. *French Review* 17: 358-60.

Giduz, Hugo. 1937. The high mortality in College Entrance French. *French Review* 10: 453-60.

Glisan, E., and J. Phillips. 1988. Foreign languages and international studies in the elementary school. *Foreign Language Annals* 21 (6): 527-34.

Goodman, Joan, Barbara Freed, and William J. McManus. 1990. Determining exemptions from foreign language requirements: Use of the

Modern Language Aptitude Test. *Contemporary Educational Psychology* 15: 131-41.

Gould, Stephen Jay. 1981. *The mismeasurement of man.* New York: Norton.

Gradman, Harry, and Bernard Spolsky. 1975. Reduced redundancy testing: A progress report. In Jones and Spolsky, *Testing language proficiency,* 59-70.

Graham, Stephen. 1978. Using the FSI Interview as a diagnostic evaluation instrument. In Clark, *Direct testing of speaking proficiency,* 31-39.

Greenleaf, Jeanne. 1929. French pronunciation tests. *Modern Language Journal* 13: 534-7.

Gumbert, Edgar, and Gail Spring. 1974. *The superschool and the superstate: American education in the twentieth century.* New York: John Wiley.

Guntermann, Gail. 1978. A study of the frequency and communicative effect of errors in Spanish. *Modern Language Journal* 62: 249-53.

Haden, Ernest, and John Stalnaker. 1934. A new type of comprehension foreign language test. *Modern Language Journal* 19: 81-92.

Haley, Sister Marie Philip. 1940. Evaluation in oral French. *Modern Language Journal* 25: 390-94.

Hall, Ernest J. 1936. Oral examinations in Spanish for undergraduates. *Hispania* 19: 461-66.

Handschin, Charles. 1919. *Handschin modern language tests.* Yonkers, NY: World Book Company.

———. 1920. Tests and measurements in modern language work. *Modern Language Journal* 4: 217-25.

———. 1940. *Modern language teaching.* Yonkers: World Book Company.

Hansen-Strain, Lynne. 1987. Cognitive style and first language background in second language test performance. *TESOL Quarterly* 21: 565-69.

Hanzeli, Victor. 1977. The effectiveness of cloze tests in measuring the competence of students of French in an academic setting. *French Review* 50: 6, 865-74.

Harris, David P. 1969. *Testing English as a foreign language.* New York: McGraw-Hill.

———. 1970. Report on an experimental group-administered Memory Span Test. *TESOL Quarterly* 4 (3): 203-13.

———. 1985. Some forerunners of cloze procedure. *Modern Language Journal* 69 (4): 367-76.

Harris, Julia. 1944. The Intensive Method at Wisconsin. *French Review* 18: 338-49.

Hayden, Phillip, M. 1920. Experience with oral examinations in modern languages. *Modern Language Journal* 5: 87-92.

Heilenman, L. Kathy. 1990. Self-assessment of second language ability: The role of response effects. *Language Testing* 7 (2): 174-201.

Hendricks, Debby, George Scholz, Random Spurling, Marianne Johnson, and Lela Vandenburg. 1980. Oral proficiency testing in an intensive English language program. In Oller and Perkins, *Research in language testing*, 77-90.

Henmon, V. A. C. 1921. *French test of vocabulary and sentence translation*. Yonkers, NY: World Book Company.

―――. 1925. Prognosis and achievement tests in the modern foreign languages. *Bulletin of the Modern Language Association of Southern California* 10: 7-11.

―――. 1926. *American Council Alpha Tests*. Yonkers, NY: World Book Company.

―――. 1929a. *Prognosis tests in the modern foreign languages*. New York: Macmillan.

―――. 1929b. *Achievement tests in the modern foreign languages*. New York: Macmillan.

Henning, Grant. 1983. Oral proficiency testing: Comparative validities of interview, imitation, and completion models. *Language Learning* 33 (3): 315-32.

―――. 1992. The ACTFL oral proficiency interview: Validity evidence. *System* 20: 365-72.

Heuser, Frederick, 1921. Regents examination in German. *Modern Language Journal* 5: 13-16.

Higgs, Theodore, ed. 1984. Teaching for proficiency: The organizing principle. Lincolnwood, IL: National Textbook Company.

Hill, Archibald ed. 1953. *Georgetown University Round Table*. Washington, DC: Georgetown University Press.

Hillegas, A. 1912. A scale for the measurement of quality in English composition. *Teachers College Record* 13: 331-86.

Hiple, David, and Joan Manley. 1987. Testing how well foreign language teachers speak: A state mandate. *Foreign Language Annals* 20 (2): 147-53.

Hosley, Deborah, and Keith Meredith. 1979. Inter- and intra-test correlates of the TOEFL. *TESOL Quarterly* 13 (2): 209-17.

Huebener, Theodore. 1944. Foreign language enrollment in the New York City high schools 1917-42. *Modern Language Forum* 28: 168-70.

Hummel, Robert D. 1985. Evaluating proficiency in comprehension skills: How can we measure what we can't observe? *ADFL Bulletin* 16 (2): 13-16.

Hunt, Kellogg W. 1965. Grammatical structures written at three grade levels. Research report, no.3. Champaign, IL: National Council of Teachers of English.

Hymes, Dell, and John Fought. 1975. *American structuralism.* The Hague: Mouton.

Ilyin, Donna. 1976. *Ilyin oral interview.* Rowley, MA: Newbury House.

Ingram, D. E. 1982. *Report on the formal trialling of the Australian Second Language Proficiency Ratings.* Canberra: Australian Department of Immigration. ERIC EDRS ED 230025.

James, Charles, ed. 1985. *Foreign language proficiency in the classroom and beyond.* Lincolnwood, IL.: National Textbook Company.

Johansson, Stig. 1975. *Papers in contrastive linguistics and language testing.* Lund University, Sweden: CWK Gleerup.

Joiner, Elizabeth. 1977. Communicative versus non-communicative practice in the teaching of beginning college French. *Modern Language Journal* 61: 236-42.

Jones, Randall. 1979. The Oral Interview of the Foreign Service Institute. In Spolsky, *Some major tests,* 104-15.

―――. 1983. Some basic considerations in testing oral proficiency. In Lee, *New Directions in language testing,* 77-84.

Jones, Randall, and Bernard Spolsky. 1975. *Testing language proficiency.* Arlington, VA: Center for Applied Linguistics. ERIC EDRS ED 107161.

Jonz, Jon. 1976. Improving on the basic egg: The m-c cloze. *Language Learning* 26 (2): 255-65.

Joynes, Edward. 1900. Dictation and composition in modern language teaching. *PMLA* 1: xxv-xxxi.

Kachru, Braj B. 1988. Teaching world Englishes. *ERIC/CLL News Bulletin* 1-8.

Kaczmarek, Celeste. 1980. Scoring and rating essay tasks. In Oller and Perkins, *Research in language testing,* 151-59.

Kalivoda, Theodore. 1970. Oral testing in secondary schools. *Modern Language Journal* 54: 328-31.

Kandel, I. L. 1936. Examinations and their substitutes in the United States. *Bulletin of the Carnegie Foundation,* no. 28.

Kaulfers, Walter. 1933a. The forecasting efficiency of current bases for prognosis in junior high school beginning Spanish. Ph.D. diss., Stanford University.

———. 1933b. Practical techniques for testing comprehension in extensive reading. *Modern Language Journal* 17: 321-27.

———. 1937. Objective tests and exercises in French revisited. *Modern Language Journal* 22: 186-90.

———. 1944. War-time developments in modern language achievement tests. *Modern Language Journal,* 28: 136-50.

Kenyon, Dorry, and Charles Stansfield. 1993. *Evaluating the efficacy of rater self-training.* Washington, DC: Center for Applied Linguistics. ERIC EDRS ED 360844.

Kirn, H. 1972. The effect of practice upon performance on dictations and cloze tests. *UCLA Workpapers in TESL* 6: 102.

Kramsch, Claire. 1986. Proficiency versus achievement: Reflections on the proficiency movement. *ADFL Bulletin* 18 (1): 22-4.

Kurz, Harry. 1934. The Librarian's Corner. *French Review* 7 (5): 339.

Lado, Robert 1946. *English test.* Ann Arbor: English Language Institute, University of Michigan.

———. 1950. Measurement in EFL with special reference to Spanish-speaking adults. Ph.D diss., University of Michigan.

———. 1951. Phonemics and pronunciation tests. *Modern Language Journal* 35: 531-42.

———. 1953. Test the language. In Hill, *Georgetown University Round Table,* 29-33.

———. 1960. English language testing: Problems of validity and administration. *English Language Teaching* 14: 153-61.

———. 1964. *Language testing.* New York: McGraw-Hill.

Lambert, Richard, ed. 1987. Foreign language instruction: A national agenda. Annals of the American Academy of Political and Social Science. Newbury Park, CA: Sage Publications.

Lange, Dale. 1987. The language teaching curriculum and a national agenda. In Lambert, *Foreign language instruction,* 70-96.

Lange, Dale, and Pardee Lowe. 1988. Rating reading passages according to the ACTFL reading proficiency standard: Can it be learned? *Foreign Language Annals* 21: 227-39.

Lantolf, James P., and William Frawley. 1985. Oral Proficiency testing: A critical analysis. *Modern Language Journal* 69 (4): 337-45.

———. 1988. Proficiency: Understanding the construct. *Studies in Second Language Acquisition* 10: 181-95.

Lapkin, Sharon, and Merrill Swain. 1977. The use of English and French cloze tests in a bilingual education program evaluation: Validity and error analysis. *Language Learning* 27: 279-314.

Larson, Jerry. 1985. *Computerized Adaptive Spanish Placement Test: Final performance report.* Washington, DC: Office of International Education. ERIC EDRS ED 355772.

Lau, Louise Margaret. 1933. The use of the Symonds Foreign Language Tests in beginning French. Master's thesis, University of Chicago.

Leavenworth, Clarence. 1926. The dictation exercise: Its variations and values. *Modern Language Journal* 10: 483-90.

Lee, James F., and Diane Musumeci. 1988. On hierarchies of reading skills and text types. *Modern Language Journal* 72 (2): 173-86.

Lee, Y. P., ed. 1983. *New directions in language testing.* Oxford: Pergamon Press.

Li, Chen-nan. 1927. Factors conditioning achievement in the modern languages. Ph.D diss., Harvard University.

Liskin-Gasparro, Judith. 1984a. The ACTFL proficiency guidelines: A historical perspective. In Higgs, ed., *Teaching for proficiency*, 11-42.

———. 1984b. The ACTFL proficiency guidelines: Gateway to testing and curriculum. *Foreign Language Annals* 17 (5): 475-89.

———. 1987. The ACTFL proficiency guidelines: An update. In Valdman, *Symposium*, 19-27.

Lococo, Veronica. 1976. *A comparison of three methods for the collection of L2 data.* Ontario, Canada: Institute for Studies in Education.

Lodeman, A. 1887. The modern languages in university, college and secondary schools. *Modern Language Notes* 1: 97-109.

Loveday, Leo. 1982. *The sociolinguistics of learning and using a non-native language.* Oxford: Pergamon Press.

Lowe, Pardee. 1985. The ILR scale as a synthesizing research principle: The view from the mountain. In James, *Foreign language proficiency*, 9-53.

———. 1987. Interagency Language Roundtable Oral Proficiency Interview. In Stansfield and Harman, *ACTFL proficiency guidelines*, 1-13.

Lowenberg, Peter. 1989. Testing English as a world language. In Alatis, *Language teaching, testing, and technology*, 216-27.

Ludwig, Jeanette. 1982. Native speaker judgments of second-language learners' efforts at communication: A review. *Modern Language Journal* 66: 274-83.

Lundeberg, Olav K. 1929. Recent developments in audition-speech tests. *Modern Language Journal* 14: 193-202.

Magnan, Sally Sieloff. 1986. Assessing speaking proficiency in the undergraduate curriculum: Data from French. *Foreign Language Annals* 19 (5): 429-38.

―――. 1988. Grammar and the ACTFL OPI: Discussion and data. *Modern Language Journal* 72 (3): 266-276.

Manning, W. H. 1987. *Development of cloze-elide tests of ESL.* Princeton: Educational Testing Service.

Major, Roy. 1987. Measuring pronunciation accuracy using computerized techniques. *Language Testing* 4 (2): 155-69.

McDonald, Katherine and James Tharp. 1938. Index to research in modern foreign language teaching. *Modern Language Journal* 23: 16-40.

Meiden, Walter. 1942. Testing in Radio Language Courses. *Modern Language Journal* 26: 55-60.

Méras, A. 1917. French examinations. *Modern Language Journal* 1: 285-301.

Mercier, Louis. 1933. Diverging trends in modern foreign language teaching and their possible reconciliation. *French Review* 6 (3): 370-86.

Miller, Minnie. 1935. A test on French life and culture. *Modern Language Journal* 19: 158-62.

Millman, Mary. 1988. The renaissance of foreign language teaching in Alabama: A case study. *Foreign Language Annals* 21 (6): 553-60.

Miner, Glenn. 1931. The measurement of achievement in Spanish. *Hispania* 14: 457-82.

Modern Language Association. 1944. *Survey of Language classes in the Army Specialized Training Program.* New York: Modern Language Association.

Monroe, W. S. 1928. Ten years of educational research, 1918-27. Bulletin. Urbana: University of Illinois.

Morello, Joseph. 1988. Attitudes of students of French toward required language study. *Foreign Language Annals* 21 (5): 435-42.

Mullen, Karen A. 1977. Rater reliability and oral proficiency evaluation. Southern Illinois University, Dept of Linguistics. ERIC EDRS ED 144403.

―――. 1978. More on cloze tests as tests of proficiency in English as a Second Language. In Brière and Hinofotis, *Concepts in language testing*, 21-32.

―――. 1979. An alternative to the cloze test. In Yorio, Perkins, and Schachter, *Tesol '79*, 187-92.

Myers, Charles T., and Richard S. Melton. 1964. A study of the relationship between scores on the MLA Proficiency Tests and ratings of teacher competence. Princeton: Educational Testing Service.

Natalicio, Diana. 1979. Repetition and dictation as language testing techniques. *Modern Language Journal* 63: 165-76.

Newmark, Maxim, ed. 1948. *Twentieth-century modern language teaching.* New York: Philosophical Library.

Nichols, Johanna. 1988. Language study, international study, and education. *Profession 88* (MLA) 10-17.

Nippold, Marilyn. 1988. *Later language development: Ages 9 through 19.* Boston: College-Hill.

Okamura, Akiko. 1995. Teachers' and nonteachers' perception of elementary learners' spoken Japanese. *Modern Language Journal* 79: 29-40.

Oller, John. 1971. Dictation as a device for testing foreign language proficiency. *English Language Teaching* 25: 254-59.

———. 1976. A program for language testing research. *Language Learning*, special issue, no.4: 141-65.

———. 1978. Pragmatics and language testing. In Spolsky, *Approaches to language testing*, 39-57.

———. 1983. *Issues in language testing research.* Rowley, MA: Newbury House.

Oller, John, Donald Bowen, Dien Ton That, and Victor Mason. 1972. Cloze tests in English, Thai, and Vietnamese: Native and nonnative performance. *Language Learning* 22 (1): 1-15.

Oller, John, and Christine Conrad. 1971. The cloze technique and ESL proficiency. *Language Learning* 21 (2): 183-95.

Oller, John, Patricia Irvine, and Parvin Atai. 1974. Cloze, dictation, and the Test of English as a Foreign Language. *Language Learning* 24 (2): 245-52.

Oller, John, and Jon Jonz. 1994. *Cloze and coherence.* Lewiston, PA: Bucknell University Press.

Oller, John, and Kyle Perkins. 1980. *Research in language testing.* Rowley, MA: Newbury House.

Oller, John, and Virginia Streiff. 1975. Dictation: A test of grammar-based expectancies. In Jones and Spolsky, *Testing language proficiency*, 71-88.

Omaggio, Alice. 1986. *Teaching language in context.* Boston: Heinle & Heinle.

Oskarsson, Mats. 1978. *Approaches to self-assessment in foreign language learning.* Oxford: Pergamon Press.

Otis, A. J. 1918. An absolute point scale for the group measurement of intelligence. *Journal of Educational Psychology* 9: 239-61, 333-48.

Paikeday, Thomas. 1987. *The native speaker is dead.* Toronto: Paikeday Publishing.

Palmer, Adrian S., and Peter Groot, eds. 1981. *The construct validation of tests of communicative competence.* Washington, DC: TESOL. ERIC EDRS ED 223103.

Palmer, Leslie, and Bernard Spolsky. 1975. *Papers on language testing, 1967-1974.* Washington, DC: TESOL.

Paquette, F. Andre, and Suzanne Tollinger. 1968. *A handbook on the MLA Foreign Language Proficiency Tests for teachers and advanced students.* New York: Modern Language Association.

Parker, William Riley. 1962. The national interest and foreign languages. New York: U.S. National Commission for UNESCO.

Parry, Thomas S., and Charles Stansfield. 1990. *Language aptitude reconsidered.* Washington, DC: Center for Applied Linguistics.

Peebles, Waldo. 1937. A test on German life and culture. *German Quarterly* 10 (1): 22-6.

Petersen, Calvin, and Francis A. Cartier. 1975. Some theoretical problems and practical solutions in proficiency test validity. In Jones and Spolsky, *Testing language proficiency,* 105-109.

Phillips, Elaine. 1992. The effect of language anxiety on students' oral test performance and attitudes. *Modern Language Journal* 76: 14-26.

Phillips, Frank. 1928. Statistical survey of education, 1925-26. Bulletin, no. 12. Washington, DC: Bureau of Education.

Phillips, June. 1988. Interpretations and misinterpretations. In *Second language proficiency assessment,* ed. Pardee Lowe and Charles Stansfield, 136-48. Englewood Cliffs: Prentice Hall.

Piazza, Linda. 1980. French tolerance of grammatical errors made by Americans. *Modern Language Journal* 64: 422-27.

Pienemann, Manfred. 1984. Psychological constraints on the teachability of languages. *Studies in Second Language Acquisition* 6: 186-214.

Pike, Lewis. 1979. An evaluation of alternative item formats for testing English as a foreign language. Princeton: Educational Testing Service.

Pimsleur, Paul. 1961. French Speaking Proficiency Test. *French Review* 34: 5-8.

———. 1966. Testing foreign language learning. In *Trends in language teaching,* ed. Albert Valdman, 175-214. New York: McGraw-Hill.

Politzer, Robert L. 1978. Errors of English speakers of German as perceived and evaluated by German natives. *Modern Language Journal* 62: 253-61.

Politzer, Robert L., and C. N. Staubach. 1961. *Teaching Spanish: A linguistic orientation.* New York: Blaisdell.

Prescott Smith, Francis. 1942. The use of standardized objective tests for sectioning French courses. *Modern Language Journal* 26 (2): 123-30.

Price, William R. 1933. "Shorn lambs"—or the New York teachers examination for oral credit. *Modern Language Journal* 18: 78-91.

Proposal for the development of a language testing program for the Peace Corps. 1970. Princeton: Educational Testing Service. ERIC EDRS ED 043024.

Radice, F. W. 1978. Using the cloze procedure as a teaching technique. *English Language Teaching* 32 (3): 201-204.

Radloff, Carla F. 1990. *Sentence repetition testing.* Arlington, TX: Summer Institute of Linguisitcs.

Raftery, Judith. 1988. Missing the mark: Intelligence testing in Los Angeles public schools, 1922-32. *History of Education Quarterly* 28 (1): 73-94.

Rand, Earl J. 1972. Integrative and discrete-point tests at UCLA. *UCLA Workpapers in TESL* 6: 67-78.

Redden, James E., ed. 1978. *Proceedings of the second international conference on frontiers in language proficiency and dominance testing.* Carbondale: Southern Illinois University.

Report of the Committee of Twelve of the Modern Language Association. 1899. Boston: D. C. Heath.

Report of the Committee on Modern Languages. 1913. Bulletin no. 41. Washington, DC: U.S. Bureau of Education.

Report of the Task Force on the Commonly Taught Languages. 1978. *ADFL Bulletin* 10 (1): 1-7.

Report to the president from the president's Commission on Foreign Language and International Studies. 1980. *Modern Language Journal* 64: 9-57.

Rice, F. A. 1959. FSI tests. *Linguistic Reporter* 1: 4.

Rice, George A. 1930. A study of achievement in foreign languages in junior and senior high school. In *Studies in modern language teaching,* 435-71. New York: Macmillan.

Richardson, H. D. 1933. Discovering aptitude for the modern languages. *Modern Language Journal* 18: 160-70.

Rifkin, Benjamin, and Felicia Roberts. 1995. Error gravity: A critical review of research design. *Language Learning* 45 (3): 511-37.

Rippa, S. A. 1964. The business community and the public schools on the eve of the Great Depression. *History of Education Quarterly* 4 (1): 33-43.

Robert, Osmond T. 1926. College entrance examinations in French. *Modern Language Journal* 11: 17-24.

———. 1927. En marge des examens d'entrée au college. *French Review* 1: 29-39.

Rogers, Agnes, and Frances Clark. 1933. Report on Bryn Mawr test of ability to understand spoken French. *Modern Language Journal* 17: 241-48.

Rugg, H. O. 1917. *Statistical methods applied to education.* Boston: Houghton Mifflin.

Russo, Giuseppe Antonio. 1940. A "quiz" on Italian civilization. *Modern Language Journal* 24 (4): 279-81.

Ryden, E. R. 1945. A GI looks at the ASTP. *Modern Language Journal* 29: 498-502.

Salomon, Ellen. 1954. A generation of prognosis testing. *Modern Language Journal* 38: 299-303.

Sammartino, Peter. 1938. A language achievement scale. *Modern Language Journal* 22: 429-32.

Savignon, Sandra. 1975. Lecture on communicative competence. University of Louisville, April. Princeton: Educational Testing Service. ERIC EDRS ED 129056.

———. 1982. Dictation as a measure of communicative competence. *Language Learning* 32 (1): 33-47.

———. 1983. *Communicative competence: Theory and classroom practice.* Reading, MA: Addison-Wesley.

———. 1985. The evaluation of communicative competence: The ACTFL provisional proficiency guidelines. *Modern Language Journal* 69 (2): 129-34.

Scharer, Rolf, and Brian North. 1992. *Towards a common European framework for reporting language competency.* Washington, DC: National Foreign Language Center.

Scheider, Rose. 1962. Evolution of the listening comprehension tests. *College Board Review* 48: 24-28.

Schulz, Renate. 1977. Discrete-point versus simulated communication testing in foreign languages. *Modern Language Journal* 61: 94-101.

Science comes to languages. 1944. *Fortune Magazine* (August) 30: 133-35, 236-40.

Seibert, Louise, and Eunice Goddard. 1931. Testing out-of-class reading. *Modern Language Journal* 15: 591-98.

Seibert, Louise, and Eunice Goddard. 1934. The use of achievement tests in sectioning students. *Modern Language Journal* 18: 289-98.

Seidner, Stanley. 1981. *Issues of language assessment.* Evanston: Illinois Board of Education.

Selinker, Larry. 1974. Interlanguage. In *Error analysis,* ed. Jack Richards, 31-54. London: Longman.

Sharma, Alex. 1981. Syntactic maturity: Assessing writing proficiency in a second language. In Proceedings of the Southern Illinois Testing Conference, Southern Illinois University, Carbondale.

Shohamy, Elana. 1983. Rater reliability of the oral interview speaking test. *Foreign Language Annals* 16 (3): 219-22.

Simms, Rochelle, and Donald Richgels. 1986. The syntactic density score revisited: Which of its components matter in the oral language of 9-15 year olds? *Language Testing* 3 (1): 39-53.

Smith, Phillip D. 1970. *A comparison of the cognitive and audiolingual approaches to foreign language instruction: The Pennsylvania Foreign Language Project.* Philadelphia: Center for Curriculum Development.

Sollenberger, Howard E. 1978. Development and current use of the FSI Oral Interview Test. In Clark, *Direct testing of speaking proficiency,* 1-12.

Spaulding, F. T. 1933. The generalists' case against modern languages. *French Review* 7 (2): 125-37.

Spiers, A.G.H. 1927. A French teacher's language scale. *French Review* 1: 13-28.

Spolsky, Bernard. 1973. What does it mean to know a language? Or how do you get someone to perform his competence? In John Oller and Jack Richards, eds., *Focus on the learner,* Rowley, MA: Newbury House, 164-76.

———, ed. 1978. *Approaches to language testing.* Arlington, VA: Center for Applied Linguistics.

———, ed. 1979. *Some major tests.* Arlington, VA: Center for Applied Linguistics.

———. 1984. A note on the dangers of terminological innovation. In *Language proficiency and academic achievement,* ed. Charlene Rivera, 41-43. Clevedon, England: Multilingual Matters.

———. 1990. The prehistory of TOEFL. *Language Testing* 7: 98-118.

————. 1993. Testing the English of foreign students in 1930. Paper presented at the Annual Language Testing Research Colloquium, Cambridge, England, August 1993. ERIC EDRS ED 368155.

Stabb, Martin. 1955. An experiment in oral testing. *Modern Language Journal* 39: 232-36.

Stalnaker, John, and Olive Eggan. 1934. The German requirements for the Ph.D. degree. *German Quarterly* 7: 69-76.

Starch, Charles 1916. *Educational measurements*. New York: Macmillan.

Starr, Wilmarth. 1962. MLA foreign language proficiency tests for teachers and advanced students. *PMLA* 77: 4, part 2, 31-41.

Stansfield, Charles. 1980. The cloze procedure as a progress test. *Hispania* 63 (4): 715-18.

————. 1981. Dictation as a measure of Spanish language proficiency. *International Review of Applied Linguistics* 19 (4): 346-51.

————. 1985. A history of dictation in foreign language teaching and testing. *Modern Language Journal* 69: 121-8.

————. 1993. Ethics, standards, and professionalism in language testing. *Issues in Applied Linguistics* 4: 189-205.

Stansfield, Charles, and Jacqueline Hansen. 1983. Field dependence-independence as a variable in second language cloze test performance. *TESOL Quarterly* 17 (1): 29-38.

Stansfield, Charles, and Chip Harman, eds. 1987. ACTFL/ETS proficiency guidelines for the less commonly taught languages: A familiarization project. Hastings-on-Hudson, NY: ACTFL. ERIC EDRS ED 289345.

Stansfield, Charles, and Dorry Kenyon. 1992. The development and validation of a simulated oral proficiency interview. *Modern Language Journal* 76: 129-41.

Stevenson, Douglas K. 1981. Beyond faith and face-validity: The multitrait-multimethod matrix and the convergent and discriminant validity of oral proficiency tests. In Palmer, *Construct validation of tests*, 37-61.

————. 1985. In other words: Language testers and translation tests. In *Translation in foreign language teaching and testing*, ed., Christopher Titford, 137-54. Tübingen: Narr.

Stevenson, Mary Lou. 1934. The use of modern language placement tests at the University of Pittsburgh. *Modern Language Journal* 18: 433-50.

Stevick, Earl. 1989. *Success with foreign languages*. Englewood Cliffs: Prenctice-Hall.

Stockwell, Robert, and J. D. Bowen. 1965. *The grammatical structures of English and Spanish*. Chicago: University of Chicago Press.

Stoddard, G. D., and G. E. Vanderbeke. 1925. *Iowa Placement Examinations*. Series FA-1, revised. Iowa City: State University of Iowa.

Stone, C. W. 1908. *Arithmetical abilities and some factors determining them.* New York: Teachers College Contributions to Education.

Stoudemire, Sterling A. 1937. Placement tests in Spanish. *Modern Language Journal* 21: 593-96.

Stubbs, Joseph, and G. Richard Tucker. 1974. The cloze test as a measure of English proficiency. *Modern Language Journal* 58: 239-41.

Sweet, Henry. 1899. *The practical study of languages.* London: Dent.

Symonds, P. 1929. A modern foreign language prognosis test. In Henmon, *Prognosis tests,* 91-126.

Taylor, Wilson. 1953. Cloze procedure: A new tool for measuring readability. *Journalism Quarterly* 30: 415-33.

Templeton, Hugh. 1977. A new technique for measuring listening comprehension. *English Language Teaching* 31 (4): 292-99.

Terman, L. 1916. *The measurement of intelligence.* Boston: Houghton-Mifflin.

Tharp, James B. 1931. The Lundeberg-Tharp Audition-Pronunciation Test in French. *Modern Language Forum* 16: 4-7.

———. 1934. A test in French civilization. *French Review* 8: 283-87.

———. 1937. Report on the New Orleans panel. *Modern Language Journal* 21: 525.

———. 1940. The College Entrance Examination Board looks at its French examination. *French Review* 13: 380-84.

Thibault, Paula. 1953. Implications of experience with College Board language tests. In Hill, *Georgetown University Round Table,* 21-29.

Thompson, Richard. 1989. Oral proficiency in the less commonly taught languages. In Alatis, *Language teaching, testing, and technology,* 228-34.

Thorndike, E. L. 1904. Introduction to the theory of mental and social measurements. New York: Teachers College.

———. 1928. The testing movement in the light of recent research. *Journal of Educational Research* 17 (5): 345-49.

Trabue, Marion. 1916. *Completion Test language scales.* New York: Teachers College.

Traxler, Arthur. 1953. The IBM Scoring Machine: An evaluation. In *Proceedings of the 1953 Invitational Conference on Testing Problems.* Princeton: Educational Testing Service.

Trotter, R. C. 1937. Relation of extensive reading and civilization. *French Review* 21: 162-64.

Ugland, Richard M. 1979. Education for victory: The high school Victory Corps and curricular adaptation during World War II. *History of Education Quarterly* 19 (4): 35-51.

Upshur, John. 1962. Language proficiency testing and the contrastive analysis dilemma. *Language Learning* 12 (2): 123-27.

———. 1971. Productive communication testing: Progress report. In *Applications of linguistics*, ed. G. E. Perren and J. L. Trim, 435-41. Cambridge: Cambridge University Press.

Valdés, Guadalupe, María Paz Echeverriarza, Enrique Lessa, and Cecilia Pino. 1988. The development of a listening skills comprehension-based program: What levels of proficiency can learners reach? *Modern Language Journal* 72 (4): 415-24.

Valdman, Albert, ed. 1987. *Proceedings of the Symposium on the Evaluation of Foreign Language Proficiency*. Indiana Universtiy, Bloomington.

Valentine, John. 1987. The College Board and the school curriculum. New York: College Entrance Examination Board.

Valette, Rebecca. 1964. The use of the dictée in the French language classroom. *Modern Language Journal* 48: 431-34.

———. 1967. *Modern language testing: A handbook*. New York: Harcourt Brace Jovanovich.

Van Ek, J. A. 1976. *Significance of the threshold level in the early teaching of modern languages*. Strasbourg: Council of Europe.

Van Lier, Leo. 1989. Oral proficiency interviews as conversations. *TESOL Quarterly* 3: 489-504.

Vann, Roberta J., Daisy E. Meyer, and Frederick Lirenz. 1984. Error gravity: A study of faculty opinion of ESL errors. *TESOL Quarterly* 18 (3): 427-40.

Wainer, Howard. 1990. *Computerized adaptive testing*. Hillsdale, NJ: Lawrence Erlbaum.

Wainman, H. 1979. Cloze testing of second language learners. *English Language Teaching* 33 (2): 126-32.

Walsh, Donald D. 1953. The College Board foreign-languages tests. *Modern Language Journal* 37: 19-22.

Weinstein, Allen. 1975. Foreign language majors: The Washington perspective. *ADFL Bulletin* 4: 18-27.

Wheeler, C. A. 1928. *Enrollment in the foreign languages in secondary schools and colleges of the United States*. New York: Macmillan.

Whiteson, Valerie, and H. Seliger. 1975. An integrative approach to the "noise test." *Audiovisual Language Journal* 13 (1): 17-18.

Wittenborn, J. R., and R. P. Larsen. 1944. A factorial study of achievement in college German. *Journal of Educational Psychology* 35: 39-48.

Wood, Ben D. 1927. *New York experiments with new-type modern language
tests.* New York: Macmillan.

————. 1956. Testing: Then and now. In *Proceedings of the ETS Invitational Conference on Testing.* Princeton: Educational Testing Service.

Woodford, Protase. 1981. *A Common metric for FLP evaluation.* Princeton:
Educational Testing Service.

Woodring, Maxie. 1925. *A study of the quality of English in Latin translations.* New York: Teachers College.

Yerkes, Robert. 1921. Psychological examining in the United States Army.
Vol. 15, *Memoirs of the National Academy of Sciences.* Washington,
DC: National Academy of Sciences.

Yorio, Carlos, Kyle Perkins, and Jacqueline Schachter. 1979. *On Tesol '79:
The learner in focus.* Washington, DC: TESOL.

Yorozvya, Ryhichi, and John Oller. 1980. Oral proficiency scales: Construct validity and the halo effect. *Language Learning* 30 (1): 135-53.